Wise Up!

Steve Reynolds and Josh Hunt

Published by Pulpit Press

Printed in the U.S.A.

All Scripture quotations, unless otherwise indicated, are taken from the *New King James Version*. Copyright © 1979, 1980, 1982 by Thomas Nelson, Inc. Used by permission. All rights reserved.

Other versions used are

CEV—*Contemporary English Version*. Copyright © 1995 by American Bible Society.

HCSB—*Holman Christian Standard Bible*. © 2001, Broadman and Holman Publishers, Lifeway Christian Resources, 127 Ninth Avenue North, Nashville, TN 37234.

ESV—Scripture taken from the *English Standard Version,* Copyright © 2001. The *ESV* and *English Standard Version* are trademarks of Good News Publishers.

KJV—Authorized King James Version.

MSG—Scripture taken from *THE MESSAGE*. Copyright © 1993, 1994 by Eugene H. Peterson. 1995, 1996, 2000, 2001, 2002. Used by permission of NavPress Publishing Group.

NASB—Scripture taken from the *New American Standard Bible,* © 1960, 1962, 1963, 1968, 1971, 1972, 1973, 1975, 1977, 1995 by The Lockman Foundation. Used by permission.

NCV—Scriptures quoted from *The Holy Bible, New Century Version,* copyright Ó 1987, 1988, 1991 by Word Publishing, Nashville, Tennessee. Used by permission.

NIV—Scripture quotations are taken from the *Holy Bible, New International Version*. *NIV* Copyright © 1973, 1978, 1984, 2011 by Biblica, Inc.™ Used by permission of Zondervan. All rights reserved worldwide. www.zondervan.com The "NIV" and "New International Version" are trademarks registered in the United States Patents and Trademark Office by Biblica, Inc.™

NIV 84—Scripture quotations are taken from the *Holy Bible, New International Version,*. 1984 edition only.

NLT—Scripture quotations marked *NLT* are taken from the *Holy Bible, New Living Translation*, copyright © 1996, 2004, 2007 by Tyndale House Foundation. Used by permission of Tyndale House Publishers, Inc., Carol Stream, Illinois 60188. All rights reserved.

NLV—Scripture taken from the *New Life Version*, © Christian Literature International.

TEV—Scripture quotations are from *Today's English Version*. Copyright © American Bible Society 1966, 1971, 1976. Used by permission.

Contents

Introduction
Wise Up!

Author Max Lucado tells the story of a wise woodcutter who once lived in a small village. Although the man was poor, he owned a beautiful white horse, and everyone who saw the animal was envious of the man's possession. People would offer him vast amounts of money for it, but the man always refused. After all, he said, to him the horse was not a possession but a friend. And how could he sell his friend?

The villagers thought the man to be incredibly foolish. "One day," they said, "someone will come along and steal your horse, and then you will have nothing." This appeared to be proven true one morning when the old man could not find the animal in his stable. "You see," said the villagers. "Someone has taken the horse. It would have been better for you if you had sold it. Now you will die in poverty."

The old man shook his head. "How can you say that the horse has been stolen? We only know that it is not in the stable. It is foolish to assume anything more." The villagers laughed, but two weeks later, the horse returned. He hadn't been stolen as the villagers thought. He had just run away into the forest, and when he came back he brought a dozen wild horses with him.

"Old man," the villagers said, "you were wise not to jump to conclusions. Now we see that the horse going missing was actually a great blessing."

The old woodcutter shook his head. "How can you say that this is a blessing? We only know that the wild horses returned with him. It is foolish to assume anything more." The villagers laughed, for they knew that with a little bit of work, the old man could train the wild horses and sell them at great profit. But a few days later, they learned that the old man's son had broken both his legs trying to do so.

"You were right," they said to him. "The wild horses have proven to be a curse. Now you have no one to help you in your old age, and you will be poorer than before."

The old man shook his head. "Once again you assume too much. We only know that my son broke his legs. Who can say if this is a blessing or a curse?" Sure enough, a few weeks later, a war broke out in the region, and all the young men in the village were required to join the army. However, because the old man's son had been injured, he was spared from the draft.

"You were right," the villagers said as they wept. "Your son's accident was a blessing. At least he is with you. Our sons are gone forever."

The old man shook his head. "I see that there is no way to reason with you, for you always jump to conclusions. Who can tell if your sons going to war will be a blessing or a curse? Who knows if they are gone forever? Only God knows."

What separated the old man from the villagers? How was he able to see past his immediate situation and not make rash decisions? The answer is that he had *wisdom*. Solomon, the wisest man who ever lived, once wrote, "Wisdom is the principal thing; therefore get wisdom. And in all your getting, get understanding. Exalt her, and she will promote you; she will bring you honor, when you embrace her" (Proverbs 4:7-8).

Solomon says that godly wisdom is to be valued above all other things in this life. Why? So that we can live well. Again and again in the Bible we read the phrase, "That it may go well with you." We are told to keep God's commands "that it may go well" with us (Deuteronomy 4:40). We are told to honor our parents "that it may be well" with us (5:16). Three times the prophet Jeremiah tells us to walk in obedience to God "that it may go well" with us (7:23; 38:20; 40:9).

Notice also that Solomon says, "Therefore *get* wisdom." We don't come into this world already possessing wisdom. In fact, we are born into this world as fools, and if we don't work to change that, we will remain fools. The apostle Paul put it this way to the believers in Corinth: "I fed you with milk and not with solid food; for until now you were not able to receive it, and even now you are still not able" (1 Corinthians 3:2).

So, how can we obtain wisdom and reap its benefits?

Getting Wisdom and Understanding

We begin the process of obtaining wisdom simply by acknowledging the fact that we don't have it—and that we won't get it if we don't work for it. We begin by realizing that wisdom won't just "ooze" into our lives and that we must go hard after it. Getting wise starts with the *desire* to get wise. As one commentator put it, "The first step in gaining wisdom is to determine that we will pursue it."[1]

Getting wisdom was Solomon's purpose in writing Proverbs, and it is our purpose for writing this book. Proverbs has always been our favorite book in the Old Testament. The proverbs are short, memorable, and apply to the everyday situations of life. Proverbs has 31 chapters, which makes it easy to read one each day. We have done this many times—memorizing certain proverbs that God has brought to our attention—and we find that our lives have been much richer for it.

People often view the commands in the Bible as "religious obligations." They see God's instructions as things He wants us to do but not things that will make our lives better. This is not a biblical perspective. As the book of Proverbs shows, God wants us to follow His instructions and gain wisdom *so that we will have a blessed life.* Again, He wants us to have wisdom so that life will go better for us.

Thomas Chalmers, a minister in the Church of Scotland, offered this keen insight: "We start changing only when we see . . . that in Christ we are not losing anything but our damnation and gaining everything we desire in our own deepest intentions. The gospel shows us Jesus pouring out his lifeblood so that we can live. The gospel says, 'Look at him. Come to him. Follow him. You will stop dying, you will start living, and it will never end.'"[2] Understanding allows us to see what we have been given in Christ. This is why Solomon says with such intensity, "In all your getting, get understanding" (Proverbs 4:7). As other versions state it, "Though

---

[1] Max Anders, *Holman Old Testament Commentary* (*Proverbs*) (Nashville, TN: Broadman & Holman Publishers, 2005).

[2] R.C. Ortlund, Jr., *Preaching the Word: Proverbs—Wisdom that Works,* "The Expulsive Power of a New Affection" (Wheaton, IL: Crossway, 2012), p. 82.

it cost all you have, get understanding" (NIV 84) and, "Whatever else you get, get understanding" (HCSB).

Understanding is the practical application of wisdom. It is wisdom with shoe leather. Wisdom and understanding go together.

An Overview of Proverbs

The main theme of Proverbs is to give us this kind of wisdom and understanding in all areas of our lives—everything from making good decisions, to relationships, to dealing with conflicts, to addictions, to money, to work, to parenting, and even to health. There are 107 verses in the book that contain the words "wise" or "wisdom."

Most of the proverbs were written by King Solomon, a man whom the Bible states "was wiser than all men" (1 Kings 4:31), though others made some contributions. For instance, the wisdom in Proverbs 25–29 comes from the men of Hezekiah, a king of Judah; Proverbs 30 comes from the wisdom of Agur; and Proverbs 31 is derived from the words of King Lemuel (or, more accurately, from his mother).

These authors wrote in a style that was widespread at the time in the ancient Near East, capturing short, concise, pithy statements of truth in a longer collection. The proverbs themselves are not promises from God but statements of the way things usually are. James Dobson states, "Proverbs were never intended to be absolute promises from God. Instead, they are probabilities of things that are likely to occur."[3]

Key Theme of Proverbs

The key theme of the book can be summed up in Proverbs 3:5-6: "Trust in the LORD with all your heart, and lean not on your own understanding; in all your ways acknowledge Him, and He shall direct your paths." Notice that Solomon says "with all your heart." The Bible has strong warnings against the half-hearted.

James wrote, "He who doubts is like a wave of the sea driven and tossed by the wind . . . he is a double-minded man, unstable in all his ways" (James 1:6, 8). In Revelation 3:16, John warned that God would spew the lukewarm out of His mouth. God wants us to be all in. Author and pastor Mark Batterson says, "We're too Christian to enjoy sin and too sinful to enjoy Christ. We've got just enough Jesus to be informed, but not enough to be transformed."[4] This should not be. Solomon admonished that we should trust in the Lord with our *whole* heart.

The next line in this passages states, "Lean not on your own understanding." Notice that Solomon doesn't say we are to turn off our understanding completely—we are just not to lean on it. God wants us to use our common sense and learn things as we go through this life. However, we are to lean on God as the source of all wisdom and recognize that His ways are higher than our ways and His thoughts are greater than our own (see Isaiah 55:9).

---

[3] Dr. James Dobson, "Will a Prodigal Child Always Return?" Dr. James Dobson's FamilyTalk. http://drjamesdobson.org/Solid-Answers/Answers?a=a4651318-9f2a-4a75-87c7-4da7b76e3ede#sthash.DZbexOYN.dpuf
[4] Mark Batterson, *Going All In: One Decision Can Change Everything* (Grand Rapids, MI: Zondervan, 2013).

As we learn to lean on God for understanding, we are also to acknowledge Him in all our ways. One of the ways we do this is through prayer. Many believers are in the habit of praying before meals. While some consider this to be just a religious ritual, a better way to think of it is simply as an opportunity to acknowledge God throughout the day. As the apostle Paul wrote, we are to "pray without ceasing, in everything give thanks" (1 Thessalonians 5:17-18). We do well to also pray about decisions and say to God, "I want to follow Your teaching and acknowledge You in all my ways."

Solomon concludes by stating that when we do these things, God will direct our paths. When we trust Him and acknowledge Him in all things, His wisdom will clear the obstacles from our course.[5] Life will never be easy, but the path will be straighter as we follow God's way.

Practical Steps

There is an old story of a young manager who asked his boss, "What is the key to wise management?" The boss replied, "Good decisions." The young man asked, "And how do you learn to make good decisions?" To this the boss replied, "Bad decisions."

It is true that if you hang around long enough and pay attention, you will eventually become wise. This is why we read in Job 12:12, "Wisdom is with aged men, and with length of days, understanding." However, there are some "shortcuts" to obtaining wisdom so that you don't have to wait until you are old. Here is a list of some practical steps you can take today to seek wisdom.

---

[5] Anders, *Holman Old Testament Commentary* (Proverbs).

- **Read the Proverbs.** Read one chapter in the book of Proverbs for each day of the month. Do this for a year, and then for the rest of your life. Rinse. Repeat.

- **Read the rest of Scripture.** Always begin the day with reading the Bible. This practice is necessary in order to live the abundant Christian life. It is a fundamental discipline of the Christian life, and there is no "living well" without it.

- **Read godly writers.** Paul wrote to young Timothy, "When you come, be sure to bring the coat I left with Carpus at Troas. Also bring my books, and especially my papers" (2 Timothy 4:13, NLT). Godly books have always been important to the people of God. It is an arrogant person who says he or she wants to read only the Bible and is willing to cut out the wisdom God has given to others.

- **Hang out with the godly.** The Bible says, "He who walks with wise men will be wise, but the companion of fools will be destroyed" (Proverbs 13:20). If you want to be wise, surround yourself with wise friends. One way to do this is to join a small group at your church and be faithful to attend it. You might also gather some friends together to study this book so that you can become wise together.

- **Accept counsel from the wise.** In Proverbs 24:6 we read, "In a multitude of counselors there is safety." All of us are smarter together than any one of us is on his or her own.

- **Fear the Lord.** The psalmist wrote, "The fear of the Lord is the beginning of wisdom; a good understanding have all those who do His Commandments" (Psalm 111:10). Solomon stated it this way: "The fear of the LORD is the beginning of wisdom, and the knowledge of the Holy One is understanding" (Proverbs 9:10).

- **Ask for wisdom.** James gave this advice to the early believers: "If any of you lacks wisdom, let him ask of God, who gives to all liberally and without reproach, and it will be given to him" (James 1:5). God is far more eager to give wisdom than we are to pursue it.

- **Apply wisdom.** God only gives wisdom to those who apply it to their lives. He does not give it merely to satisfy our intellectual curiosity. Solomon wrote, "My son, do not forget my law, but let your heart keep my commands" (Proverbs 3:1). If we say to God, "Give me Your opinion and I will decide what I will do," we will only find heaven to be silent.

- **Value wisdom.** Finally, we must value wisdom. Treasure it. Honor it. It is more valuable than anything else we could obtain.

Reflect on this last point for a moment. How important is it to you to get wisdom? Would you say it is the principal thing in your life? Do you truly value it? Is getting wisdom is your primary objective? We know that this is the way Solomon saw it. He said obtaining wisdom is the "most important thing you can do" (TEV).

The Best Question Ever

In Proverbs 4:8, Solomon tells us to *exalt* wisdom. That is what we seek to do in this book. If we accomplish nothing else, we hope we leave you with a profound appreciation for the central importance of getting wisdom. Andy Stanley calls this "the best question ever." As we go through our day, the best question is not whether it feels good, or if we can afford it, or if this person is the right one for us, or if we should stay or leave. No, the best question ever is, "Is it wise?"

Solomon also says that we are to *embrace* wisdom. We are to love it. The *English Standard Version* states it, "Prize her highly." The verse goes on to tell us why: "So that she will promote you." Again, this is a reminder that pursuing wisdom is *good for us*. Life is better if we pursue wisdom. Good things come to people who are wise.

So, are you ready to seek wisdom—using the book of Proverbs as your guide—and commit to apply that knowledge to your life? Are you ready to live the life that God has for you—"that it may go well with you"? If so, you are ready to look at the first of 10 areas that we will examine as to where wisdom is to be applied. We will begin by looking at our decision-making.

Wise Up About Decisions

On March 31, 1909, the company of Harland & Wolff, based in Belfast, Ireland, began construction on a monumental ship. The size of this craft had never been attempted before, and the company had to create an entirely new shipway to accommodate it. The builders constructed the craft by placing thousands of one-inch-thick steel plates secured by two million wrought-iron rivets to the hull. The ship was equipped with the latest technology and heralded as being "virtually unsinkable."

However, a poor decision by the company executives doomed the craft from the start. As the building progressed, Harland & Wolff came under pressure to finish the ship more quickly than planned. In response to this demand, the company decided to order wrought iron that was one level below the quality generally specified for rivets. In addition, the company resorted to using suppliers that were not certified to provide these materials. Later examinations revealed that the rivets contained an average of three times more slag than was acceptable at the time. The company also ordered workers to place two rows of rivets in the main hull section, instead of three rows.

When this ship hit an iceberg during its maiden voyage on the morning of April 15, 1912, the rivets snapped off and six compartments flooded. In just two and a half hours, the mighty Titanic sunk and fell to the bottom of the ocean. Harland & Wolff's decision proved to be one of the deadliest maritime disasters in modern history, as 1,523 met their end in the frigid water. If the iron rivets had been of higher quality, or if the company had opted for more rows of rivets in the hull, it is likely that fewer compartments would have flooded. This would have at least bought time for the Carpathia, which was four hours away, to arrive on the scene and rescue passengers.[6]

Many people today make decisions as if there were no consequences for tomorrow. They respond to pressure from others or just decide to take what seems to be the "easy way" out of a problem. They are fond of the philosophy that if something feels good, they should do it. However, as the story of Harland & Wolff and the Titanic shows, *decisions do matter.* The decisions we make today *will* determine the life we live tomorrow . . . and forever.

Where we are today is a result of the decisions we made or the decisions that were made by people around us. Andy Stanley calls this the "principle of the path." He writes, "The direction you are currently traveling—relationally, financially, spiritually, and the list goes on and on—will determine where you end up in each of those respective arenas. This is true regardless of your goals, your dreams, your wishes, or your wants. . . . Like every principle, you can leverage this one to your advantage or ignore it to your disadvantage. Just as there are paths that have led us to places we never intended to be, there are paths that lead us away from those places as well."[7]

Our decisions determine our destiny. So, how do we make wise decisions? Before we can answer that question, we first need to examine what wisdom in decision-making is and what it is not.

---

[6] "What Really Sank the Titanic?" Elsevier Materials Today, September 28, 2008. http://www.materialstoday.com/metals-alloys/news/what-really-sank-the-titanic/
[7] Andy Stanley, *The Principle of the Path: How to Get from Where You Are to Where You Want to Be* (Nashville, TN: Thomas Nelson, 2008).

What Is Wisdom in Decision-Making?

Wisdom in decision-making does not come about as a result of education. Although education is a good thing, a person can have as many degrees as a thermometer and still be thoroughly foolish. For example, my (Steve) mom and dad never graduated from high school, but I would put their wisdom up against anyone I know. They are wise in the things of God because they have meditated on Scripture and followed His ways.

In the Bible, we get a picture of the world's wisdom through an unusual request made by the mother of James and John, two of Jesus' disciples. She approached Christ and said, "Grant that these two sons of mine may sit, one on Your right hand and the other on the left, in Your kingdom" (Matthew 20:21). Her request represents the wisdom of the world, which tells us "the early bird gets the worm" and we should always seek to be first and better than others. But Jesus said, "Whoever desires to become great among you, let him be your servant" (verse 26).

The way of the world and the way of godly wisdom are exactly opposite. In Proverbs 14:12 we read, "There is a way that seems right to a man, but its end is the way of death." As a pastor, I have people come into my office nearly every week and say, "This just *seems* like the right thing to do." Just because something *seems* right doesn't mean it *is* right or will lead to the place where you want to go.

True wisdom is not based on human intellect or education but comes from *knowing and doing the will of God*. Notice the two parts: "knowing" and "doing." In Ephesians 5:15-17, Paul writes, "See then that you walk circumspectly, not as fools but as wise, redeeming the time, because the days are evil. Therefore do not be unwise, but understand what the will of the Lord is." For Paul, wisdom involved understanding the will of God and walking "circumspectly," or walking according to the will of God. *The Message* version reads, "Watch your step." One commentator likens this circumspection to a cat walking on a wall into which pieces of glass are embedded.[8]

In verse 16, Paul also states that we are to make "the most of every opportunity" (NIV). John MacArthur says, "It is common not to finish what we begin. Sometimes a symphony is unfinished, a painting uncompleted, or a project left half-done because the musician, painter, or worker dies. But usually it is simply the death of a person's commitment that causes the incompletion. Dreams never become reality and hopes never materialize because those working toward them never get beyond the first few steps. For many people, including many Christians, life can be a series of unfinished symphonies. Even in the familiar opportunities of everyday Christian living, those who are truly productive have mastered the use of the hours and days of their lives."[9]

What Motivates a Wise Person?

True wisdom means walking according to the will of God, so it only makes sense that a truly wise person is motivated by the things of God. Wise people have a long-term perspective. They "store up choice food and olive oil" for tomorrow, while foolish people "gulp theirs down" (Proverbs 21:20, NIV). They work to secure joy throughout their lives and throughout eternity, while the foolish work to secure joy for the weekend. The wise plan for the future to obtain happiness, while the foolish mortgage the future, to obtain

---

[8] Stuart Olyott, *Alive in Christ: Ephesians Simply Explained* (Darlington, UK: Evangelical Press, 1994), p. 118.

[9] John MacArthur, *The MacArthur New Testament Commentary: Ephesians* (Chicago: Moody Press, 1986), p. 221.

the pleasures of today. The wise choose "to suffer affliction with the people of God" rather than "enjoy the passing pleasures of sin" (Hebrews 11:25).

In his book *The Unheavenly City*, sociologist Dr. Edward Banfield of Harvard University conducted one of the most profound studies ever done on success and priority setting. Banfield's goal was to find out how and why some people become financially independent during the course of their working lifetimes. He started off convinced that the answer would be found in factors such as family background, education, intelligence, or influential contacts. However, what he discovered was that a person's success was primarily due to a particular attitude in his or her mind.

Banfield called this the "long-time perspective." In his study, the men and women who were the most successful and the most likely to move up economically were those who took the future into consideration with every decision they made in the present. The longer that people took to consider their options during a time of planning, the more likely it was that they would achieve greatly during their career.[10] This is the way of wisdom: take an eternal view of life.

What Does a Wise Person Value?

Not only do wise people consider the long-term implications in their decision-making, but they also consider the value of wisdom itself. Solomon was deemed the wisest person who ever lived because he *valued wisdom*.

---

[10] Brian Tracy, "The Key to Long-term Success," Get Motivation. http://getmotivation.com/articlelib/articles/brian_tracy_long_term_success.htm

Imagine if God were to come to you one day and say, "Ask Me for anything and I will give it to you" (2 Chronicles 1:7, NLV). What would you request? Look at Solomon's response: "O LORD God . . . give me wisdom and knowledge, that I may go out and come in before this people; for who can judge this great people of Yours?" (verses 9-10). Solomon understood two things: (1) wisdom was valuable, and (2) he didn't have it. He knew that he was in over his head, and he was feeling overwhelmed with the task. God will do that to us. He will test us and stretch us, and as the years go by, the tests will get more difficult—not less.

Wisdom always starts at this point. It begins when we understand that we are not wise but need to be. It starts when we humbly go to God and acknowledge our deficiency. James wrote, "God opposes the proud but shows favor to the humble" (4:6). God runs to the humble. He draws near to all who seek Him. He is eager to give wisdom to those who acknowledge their need for it and seek it.

This was certainly true in Solomon's case, and God rewarded him for it. The Lord said to him, "Because this was in your heart, and you have not asked riches or wealth or honor or the life of your enemies, nor have you asked long life . . . wisdom and knowledge are granted to you; and I will give you riches and wealth and honor, such as none of the kings have had who were before you, nor shall any after you have the like" (2 Chronicles 1:11-12).

Notice that verse 11 says God *looks at the heart*. God knows if we want to follow Him or not. I love the saying, "We are about as close to God as we want to be." God is a perfect gentleman, and if we want Him to stay far way, He will do so. However, when we ask Him to come into our lives, He will come running back to us like the father in the parable of the Prodigal Son (see Luke 15:20).

God saw into the heart of Solomon and granted his request. "God gave Solomon wisdom and exceedingly great understanding, and largeness of heart like the sand on the seashore. Thus Solomon's wisdom excelled the wisdom of all the men of the East and all the wisdom of Egypt. For he was wiser than all men . . . and his fame was in all the surrounding nations. He spoke three thousand proverbs, and his songs were one thousand and five. . . . And men of all nations, from all the kings of the earth who had heard of his wisdom, came to hear the wisdom of Solomon" (1 Kings 4:29-32, 34).

What Are the Benefits of Wisdom?

Wisdom is more valuable than money, more precious than gold, and even better than winning the lottery. When we value wisdom, it adds value to our lives. In Proverbs 3:13-18, Solomon lists just some of the benefits we will receive when we seek wisdom:

> Happy is the man who finds wisdom, and the man who gains understanding; for her proceeds are better than the profits of silver, and her gain than fine gold. She is more precious than rubies, and all the things you may desire cannot compare with her. Length of days is in her right hand, in her left hand riches and honor. Her ways are ways of pleasantness, and all her paths are peace. She is a tree of life to those who take hold of her, and happy are all who retain her.

Let's take a look at each of the benefits that Solomon says will come to those who humbly seek wisdom from God.

Happiness (Proverbs 3: 13, 18)

Solomon starts and ends this passage by pointing out the link between wisdom and happiness. If we lead a wise life, we will lead a happy life. Unfortunately, the opposite is also true. If we fail to find wisdom, we will lead a frustrating and miserable life.

Science has confirmed that those who seek God's wisdom are happier in life. According to a study by the Pew Research Center, "People who attend religious services weekly or more are happier (43% very happy) than those who attend monthly or less (31%); or seldom or never (26%). This correlation between happiness and frequency of church attendance has been a consistent finding . . . over the years."[11]

Notice in verse 18 that Solomon states, "Happy are all who retain [wisdom]." We know from 1 Kings 11 that Solomon found wisdom but did not retain it. He started well, but he intermarried with foreign women in violation of God's commands. Ultimately, when Solomon was old, his many wives influenced him to turn his heart after other gods, "and his heart was not loyal to the LORD his God, as was the heart of his father David" (verse 4). Christian living is about finishing well. In the words of Eugene Peterson, it is "a long obedience in the same direction."[12]

Longevity (Proverbs 3:16a)

Longevity was one of the benefits that God gave to Solomon because he asked for wisdom, and there are many other passages in the Bible that address this link. In Deuteronomy 6:2, Moses told the people to "keep all God's statutes and His commandments . . . that your days may be prolonged." In Proverbs 28:16 we read, "A ruler

---

[11] "Are We Happy Yet?" Pew Research Social and Demographic Trends, February 13, 2006. http://www.pewsocialtrends.org/2006/02/13/are-we-happy-yet/
[12] Eugene Peterson, *A Long Obedience in the Same Direction* (Downers Grove, IL: InterVarsity Press, 2000).

who lacks understanding is a great oppressor, but he who hates covetousness will prolong his days."

Once again, modern research proves that what the Bible says is true. According to a study published in the *Journal of Gerontology,* people who go to church regularly live longer than those who do not. During the six-year study, researchers examined 4,000 residents of North Carolina between the ages of 64 and 101 and found that those who attended religious services at least once per week were 46 percent less likely to die. According to lead author Harold G. Koenig, MD, when controls were put in place for age, race, level of sickness and other health and social factors, "there was still a 28 percent reduction in mortality." Koenig compared the difference in mortality rates between churchgoers and non-churchgoers to smokers and non-smokers.[13]

Wealth (Proverbs 3:16b)

The Bible in general—and the Proverbs in particular—has a great deal to say about the benefits of managing money wisely. In fact, Jesus talked about money more than any other subject. Of His roughly 40 parables, nearly half speak directly about money, and many others touch on material wealth. In the book of Acts, we read that among the early believers there was no one in need financially, "for all who were possessors of lands or houses sold them, and brought the proceeds of the things that were sold, and laid them at the apostles' feet; and they distributed to each as anyone had need" (4:34-35). Missiologists refer to this concept as "redemption and lift." The term describes the upward mobility of those whose lives are

---

[13] "Spirituality May Help People Live Longer," WebMD. http://www.webmd.com/balance/features/spirituality-may-help-people-live-longer

bettered in every way as a direct result of their new birth—not only spiritually but also socially and economically.[14]

Honor (Proverbs 3:16c)

Honor is a clear benefit of wisdom. After all, who doesn't respect a wise person, and who does respect a fool? In Proverbs 22:1 we read, "A good name is to be chosen rather than great riches, loving favor rather than silver and gold." Obtaining wisdom will always bring us respect and honor.

Pleasure (Proverbs 3:17a)

Exhibiting wisdom will make all of life better, while being foolish will make all of life worse. As Raymond C. Ortlund notes, "Money can put food on the table, but wisdom puts laughter around that table. Money can buy a house, but wisdom makes it a home. Money can buy a woman jewelry, but wisdom wins her heart."[15]

Peace (Proverbs 3:17b)

In Philippians 4:6-7, Paul writes, "Be anxious for nothing, but in everything by prayer and supplication, with thanksgiving, let your requests be made known to God; and the peace of God, which surpasses all understanding, will guard your hearts and minds through Christ Jesus." Wisdom will enable us to lay hold of a life of peace.

---

[14] Peter Barfoot, "Redemption and Lift," Spirituality.org, April 16, 20101. http://spirituality.org.au/?p=415
[15] Raymond C. Ortlund, Jr, *Preaching the Word: Proverbs—Wisdom that Works* (Wheaton, IL: Crossway, 2012), p. 75.

So, in the end, we see that wisdom will help both the quality and quantity of our lives. It will enable us to live longer, fuller, richer, and better.

Get Wise!

Solomon concludes, "Get wisdom. Though it cost all you have, get understanding" (Proverbs 4:7, NIV). The meaning is clear.

Whatever else you do, get wisdom.

Whatever it costs you, get wisdom.

However much time it takes, get wisdom.

Again, the good news is that God is *eager* to make you wise. He is a God of all wisdom, and He desires to share His immense wisdom with you. "For the LORD gives wisdom; from His mouth come knowledge and understanding; He stores up sound wisdom for the upright; He is a shield to those who walk uprightly; He guards the paths of justice, and preserves the way of His saints" (Proverbs 2:6-8).

Wise Up About Communication

The quality of our lives is mostly about the quality of our relationships, and the quality of our relationships is mostly about the quality of our communication. Solomon understood this well when he wrote, "Death and life are in the power of the tongue, and those who love it will eat its fruit" (Proverbs 18:21). Our tongue— our words—can change other people's lives for the better or for the worse.

Sophia Hawthorne also understood this principle. In April 1846, her husband, Nathaniel, who had shown great promise as writer, was appointed to a government position at the Salem Custom House in Massachusetts. While the pay was good for the time, the job made it difficult for him to pursue his writing. As he complained to his friend Henry Wadsworth Longfellow, "I find myself dreaming about stories, as of old; but these forenoons in the Custom House undo all that the afternoons and evenings have done. I should be happier if I could write."[16]

The story is told that in June 1849, three years after the birth of the couple's second child, Nathaniel lost his job due to a political change in Washington, DC. He came home heartbroken and defeated, but Sophia surprised him by reacting to the news with joy. "Now you can write your book!" she said.

---

[16] Edwin H. Miller, *Salem Is My Dwelling Place: A Life of Nathaniel Hawthorne* (Iowa City, IA: University of Iowa Press, 1991), p. 265.

Nathaniel wasn't so sure. "And what shall we live on while I'm writing it?" he asked. To his amazement, Sophia opened a drawer and revealed a wad of money she had saved out of her housekeeping budget—enough to last a year. "I always knew you were a man of genius," she told him. "I always knew you'd write a masterpiece."

With Sophia's support, Nathaniel began work on what would become *The Scarlet Letter*. When the book was released in 1850, it sold 2,500 copies in 10 days—a staggering amount for the time— and secured the family's financial future for next decade. The publication of *The Scarlet Letter* ushered in Nathaniel's most lucrative period as a writer.

Sophia believed in her husband, spoke life-giving words to him, and refused to allow him to become discouraged. As a result, almost every library in America today has a copy of *The Scarlet Letter* on its shelves.[17]

The novelist William Edwards Norris wrote, "If your lips would keep from slips,
five things take note with care; to whom you speak, of whom you speak, and how, and when, and where." Ask friends who were once close what pulled them apart and you will nearly always find it was because of their communication.

There is an old saying that "sticks and stones can break my bones, but words can never hurt me," but that is a lie. Words can hurt deeply. The tongue is the only boneless part of the body that can break a lot of bones. It wields immense power for good or evil. James wrote, "The tongue is a small part of the body, but it makes

---

[17] Harvey Mackay, *Use Your Head to Get Your Foot in the* Door (New York: Penguin Books, 2010).

great boasts. Consider what a great forest is set on fire by a small spark" (James 3:5, NIV).

So, given the immense power of our words, how do we wise up about our communication?

Speak Less

The first way we show wisdom with our communication is simply to speak less. Earlier in his letter, James wrote, "Everyone should be quick to listen, slow to speak and slow to become angry" (1:19, NIV). Perhaps he had spent time meditating on these proverbs:

> In the multitude of words sin is not lacking, but he who restrains his lips is wise (Proverbs 10:19).

> Even a fool is counted wise when he holds his peace; when he shuts his lips, he is considered perceptive (Proverbs 17:28).

> The tongue of the wise uses knowledge rightly, but the mouth of fools pours forth foolishness (Proverbs 15:2).

Notice that last verse. In the *New International Version,* it reads, "The tongue of the wise adorns knowledge, but the mouth of the fool gushes folly." James says we need to be slow to speak and quick to listen, but so many of us get the order wrong. We are quick to become angry, and the words we speak in our rage bring death instead of life. If we want to sin less than we do, all we need to do is talk less than we do.

We don't always have to get the last word in and "win" the argument. Silence can say much and even make a fool seem wise. As the old adage states, "It is better to remain silent and be thought a fool than to speak out and remove all doubt."

Speak the Right Words at the Right Time

We also wise up about our communication when we speak the right words at the right time. Solomon writes, "A word spoken in due season, how good it is. . . . A word fitly spoken is like apples of gold in settings of silver" (Proverbs 15:23; 25:11). Words fitly spoken "in due season" can encourage others and bring them life.

Charles Swindoll sums up this idea when he states, "Like Jell-O, concepts assume the mold of the words into which they are poured. Who has not been stabbed awake by the use of a particular word . . . or combinations of words? Who has not found relief from a well-timed word spoken at the precise moment of need? Who has not been crushed beneath the weight of an ill-chosen word? And who has not gathered fresh courage because a word of hope penetrated the fog of self-doubt? The term 'word' remains the most powerful of all four-letter words. Colors fade. Shorelines erode. Temples crumble. Empires fall. But 'a word fitly spoken' endures."[18]

If we want to be wise with our words, we need to learn to speak the right things at the right times.

Listen to Both Sides of the Story

Newscaster Walter Cronkite once famously said, "In seeking truth you have to get both sides of the story." What is true in journalism is also true in life. If you want to get to the heart of a situation and really know what is going on, you have to hear out both sides.

---

[18] Charles Swindoll, *Wisdom for the Way: Wise Words for Busy People* (Nashville, TN: Thomas Nelson, 2007).

Solomon makes this astute observation: "The first one to plead his cause seems right, until his neighbor comes and examines him" (Proverbs 18:17). We see this illustrated in every episode of *Law and Order* and other courtroom dramas. When the prosecutor stands up and makes his or her case, the words always sound compelling. However, everything changes when the defense attorney steps up to offer his or her side on the case. The same is true in political debates—one candidate seems persuasive until we hear the other side.

Every story sounds good until you receive another perspective on it. We have to learn to be "quick to listen" so we consider both sides and don't rush to judgment.

Don't Stir Up Trouble

When James states that the tongue is like a small spark that can set a forest on fire (see 3:5), he is referring to the damage that can be caused by words spoken to stir up trouble. Proverbs has much to say on the subject: "Do not strive with a man without cause, if he has done you no harm. . . . A perverse man sows strife, and a whisperer separates the best of friends. . . . As charcoal is to burning coals, and wood to fire, so is a contentious man to kindle strife" (3:30; 16:28; 26:21).

Some people are just hard to get along with. They like to stir up trouble and enjoy antagonizing others. Rick Warren, bestselling author and pastor of Saddleback Church, calls these "EGR" people—"Extra Grace Required." Every church, small group, and Sunday School class have these types of individuals. They are rough around the edges. They are a bit rude. They don't have good manners all the time. Sometimes they don't shower every day.

Don't be an EGR person. Choose to be wise and get along with others. Jesus said, "Blessed are the peacemakers, for they shall be called sons of God" (Matthew 5:9). Always seek to smooth things over and bring peace rather than ruffling things up.

Don't Listen to Rumors

The best way to ensure that we do not cause conflict with our words is to not gossip about others and to not listen to rumors. Once again, Proverbs has much to say on the subject: "The words of a talebearer are like tasty trifles, and they go down into the inmost body. . . . He who goes about as a talebearer reveals secrets; therefore do not associate with one who flatters with his lips. . . . Where there is no wood, the fire goes out; and where there is no talebearer, strife ceases" (18:8; 20:19; 26:20).

The Hebrew word for "talebearer" in these verses is translated "complainer" in other passages. It involves more than just not *talking* about another person but also not *complaining* about him or her. We are not to associate with these individuals or partake of their "tasty trifles." God tells us in Exodus 23:1 not to "circulate a false report" or join in "with the wicked to be an unrighteous witness."

When in doubt, consider this test. If the person were sitting next to you, would you still join in the conversation? Would you listen to what is being said about that person and respond in the same way? If you would not, it is likely you are listening to the words or a talebearer and are spreading gossip.

Watch Your Tone

We must not only be wise about the content of our conversations but also about the tone of our speech. Solomon tells us, "A soft answer turns away wrath, but a harsh word stirs up anger" (Proverbs 15:1). Notice that he says "a soft answer," not a "right answer." What we are saying to others might be totally correct, but we can still stir up wrath if we are judgmental or overbearing in our communication. As Paul tells us, we are to speak "the truth in love" (Ephesians 4:15).

In his book *Blink,* Malcolm Gladwell discusses a recent study that was done comparing a group of doctors. The researchers in the study began by selecting 10-second audio clips from a group of doctors who had been sued by their patients and 10-second clips from those who had not. Just to make things more interesting, the researchers garbled the recordings so that only the doctors' tone of voice could be perceived. They discovered that they could predict with a high degree of accuracy those surgeons who had been sued.

According to Gladwell, the researchers were stunned to find that what determined whether a doctor would be sued was not incompetence but simply his or her tone of voice. "The judges knew nothing about the skill level of the surgeons," he writes. "They didn't know how experienced they were, what kind of training they had, or what kind of procedures they tended to do. They didn't even know what the doctors were saying to their patients. All they were using for their prediction was their analysis of the surgeon's tone of voice."[19]

---

[19] Malcolm Gladwell, *Blink: The Power of Thinking Without Thinking* (New York: Little, Brown and Company, 2005).

Accept Correction

Another way to be wise in our communication is to humbly accept correction when we are in the wrong. Solomon writes, "Poverty and shame will come to him who disdains correction, but he who regards a rebuke will be honored. . . . The ear that hears the rebukes of life will abide among the wise" (Proverbs 13:18; 15:31). Do-it-yourself Christianity doesn't work. It is not enough for us to read our Bibles, pray, and attend church. We need people in our lives that know us, love us, and have the courage to correct us, and we need the grace to listen when they do.

Get Wise!

We must always remember that our words have power. We can choose to use words that are like "choice silver" or are "worth little" (Proverbs 10:20). We can be righteous and "bring forth wisdom" or have perverse tongues that "will be cut out" (Proverbs 10:31). Our speech can be "like the piercings of a sword" or can "promote health" (Proverbs 12:18). Our communication can bring life or death. It can build up or tear down.

So speak wisely. Listen intently. Wise up and live well.

Wise Up
About Friendships

The quality of the people we choose to be our friends can have a lasting impact on our lives. One of the clearest examples of this that we find in the Bible is in the story of Rehoboam in 1 Kings 12. Rehoboam was the son of Solomon and heir to the throne of Israel. When he became king at the age of 41, the nation's leaders gathered for his coronation and requested that he ease some of the tax burdens that Solomon had placed on the nation. The people of Israel were evidently tired of bearing the cost of his father's massive palaces and public works projects.

Rehoboam met the delegation, said that he would consider their request, and told them to return three days later to hear his answer. When they had departed, he first met with the elders of his court who had served under his father, Solomon. These wise men said to Rehoboam, "If you will be a servant to these people today, and serve them, and answer them, and speak good words to them, then they will be your servants forever" (1 Kings 12:7).

Rehoboam didn't care for this advice, so he next consulted with the young men who had grown up with him. These foolish men told the king, "Thus you should speak to this people who have spoken to you . . . 'Whereas my father put a heavy yoke on you, I will add to your yoke; my father chastised you with whips, but I will chastise you with scourges!'" (verses 10-11). Rehoboam enjoyed all of the luxurious buildings and public works his father had created, so he agreed.

The result was disastrous. Ten of the 12 tribes rebelled and formed the northern kingdom of Israel, with the remaining tribes in the south forming the kingdom of Judah. Never again, until modern times, would the nation be united. The two kingdoms remained in a state of war throughout Rehoboam's 17-year reign.

As we saw in the last chapter, the quality of our lives is mostly about the quality of our relationships. A good friend can lift us up, encourage us, set us on the right path, and lead us into wisdom. A poor friend can tear us down, discourage us, set us on the wrong path, and lead us into foolishness. For this reason, we need to find the right friends and learn how to be good friends ourselves.

Find the Right Friends

Solomon wrote, "He who walks with wise men will be wise, but the companion of fools will be destroyed" (Proverbs 13:20). There are certain relationships that we make by choice, while others come by circumstance. For instance, we can choose with whom we spend our free time, but we can't pick our family members or usually even our coworkers. When the Bible speaks of "walking with" others, it refers to the choices we make in relationships. If we choose wise people as our friends, we will become wise. Conversely, if we choose friends who are fools, we are fools (or soon will be).

As the story of Rehoboam illustrates, we are all profoundly influenced by the behavior of the people around us. Behavior is contagious. For instance, studies show that if the spouse of a smoker quits, that person is 67 percent more likely to also quit.[20] Other studies show that obesity is contagious, as is losing weight.

In the 2009 Shape Up Rhode Island campaign, 3,300 overweight or obese individuals were placed on teams averaging between 5 to 11 members each. The teams were allowed to compete against other teams in three categories: weight loss, physical activity, and pedometer steps. At the end of the 12-week campaign, there was a clear correlation between weight loss and the team on which the overweight/obese person had been placed. Those who lost at least five percent of their initial body weight tended to be on the same teams, and those who were on teams competing in the weight loss category lost greater amounts of weight. Participants who reported they had been influenced by their teammates were 20 percent more likely to achieve this significant weight loss.[21]

Even teen pregnancy is contagious. In one study, researchers found that if a teenage girl had an older sister who became pregnant, she was twice as likely to get pregnant herself.[22] It is not all that difficult to understand why. If a teen's older sister gets pregnant, getting pregnant becomes her new "normal." It is no longer a shocking scandalous thing that "those people" do—it now becomes something that she and her family does. We are profoundly affected by the behavior of those whom we consider to be "our people."

[20] Charles W. Bryant, "Is Quitting Smoking Contagious?" How Stuff Works. http://health.howstuffworks.com/wellness/smoking-cessation/quitting-smoking-contagious1.htm
[21] "Weight Loss Can Be Contagious, Study Suggests," LifeSpan, February 14, 2012. http://www.sciencedaily.com/releases/2012/02/120214122124.htm
[22] "Teenage Pregnancy Is 'Contagious,'" BBC News, August 9, 2011. http://www.bbc.co.uk/news/health-14442709

In Galatians 6:7, Paul writes, "Do not be deceived, God is not mocked; for whatever a man sows, that he will also reap." If we hang around people who influence us to do foolish things, we will reap the negative consequences of our actions. However, if we spend our time with people who are wise, we will be influenced to take wise actions. We reap what we—and our friends—sow into our lives.

So, how do we ensure that we are picking the right friends, and how can we ourselves be a good influence on others? The book of Proverbs gives us several steps we can take to exercise wisdom in our relationships.

Be Kind to Your Friends

The first step is pick friends who are kind and to be kind ourselves. Solomon summed this up when he wrote, "What is desired in a man is kindness" (Proverbs 19:22a). The phrase "What is desired in a man" can literally be translated, "What makes a man attractive" (NLT). The term "kindness" in this verse is a strong word for a type of covenant loyalty that is typically used of God. It can also be translated as "lovingkindness," "love," or "mercy," as we find in Psalm 136:

> Oh, give thanks to the LORD, for He is good!
> For His *mercy* endures forever.
> Oh, give thanks to the God of gods!
> For His *mercy* endures forever.
> Oh, give thanks to the Lord of lords!
> For His *mercy* endures forever.

Researchers have actually found that kindness is more attractive to people than good looks. In a study conducted on more than 10,000 young adults from 33 different countries, researchers found that universally, without exception, people most prefer kindness in a mate. It ranked higher in people's minds that either good looks or a prospective mate's financial prospects.[23] Other research shows that being kind can lead to the following beneficial results:

- **It makes us happier:** On a biochemical level, it is believed that the good feeling we get from being kind is caused by elevated levels of endogenous opioids, the brain's natural version of morphine. These cause elevated levels of dopamine, often referred to as the "helper's high."

- **It gives us healthier hearts:** Acts of kindness can produce the hormone oxytocin in the brain and the body. This chemical causes the release of nitric oxide in blood vessels, which dilates (expands) the blood vessels, reduces blood pressure, and in turn protects the heart. Because acts of kindness can produce oxytocin, we could say that kindness itself is "cardio-protective."

- **It slows aging:** Two culprits that speed the process of aging are free radicals and inflammation, both of which result from making unhealthy lifestyle choices. However, oxytocin, the chemical we just examined, reduces levels of free radicals and inflammation in the cardiovascular system, thus slowing the aging process at its source. (Incidentally, these two culprits also play a major role in heart disease, which is another reason why kindness is good for the heart.)

- **It makes for better relationships:** Kindness reduces the emotional distance between two people and makes them feel bonded. It's a trait so strong in humans that

---

[23] David R. Hamilton, PhD, *Why Kindness is Good for You* (London: Hay House UK, 2010).

it's actually carried in the genes. We are literally wired for kindness.

- **It is contagious.** Just as behaviors are contagious, so is kindness. When we're kind we inspire others to be kind, which creates a ripple effect that can spread outward to three degrees of separation.[24] In one case, when an anonymous person walked into a clinic and donated a kidney, it set off a pay-it-forward effect that led to other people donating their kidneys to someone in need. The domino effect of this one act of kindness spanned the length and breadth of the United States, leading to 10 people receiving a new kidney in one year as a consequence of that anonymous donor.[25]

We live in a mean world. Every day we have to deal with mean drivers, mean emails, and mean people on the street. If only everyone would heed the wisdom of Ephesians 4:32, one of the first verses I (Josh) memorized. In the old *King James Version* that I learned, it reads, "Be ye kind to one another." This is sage advice. We want to be a friend who is kind and find friends who are kind.

Words of kindness need to be spoken out loud. This is something I have been working on in my own life. I sometimes have kind thoughts, but I tend to leave them there in my head and not verbalize them. Note that this doesn't have to be anything elaborate. The other day I passed by a couple of guys in the hall and commented to them on how sharply dressed they looked. Acts of kindness can be as simple as that. Just speak a kind word and make your world a better place.

---

[24] David R. Hamilton, PhD, "Five Beneficial Side Effects of Kindness," Huffington Post, June 2, 2011. http://www.huffingtonpost.com/david-r-hamilton-phd/kindness-benefits_b_869537.html

[25] "Stranger Kidney Swap Chain Has Potential," CBS News, March 11, 2009. http://www.cbsnews.com/news/stranger-kidney-swap-chain-has-potential/

Be Cheerful Around Your Friends

Proverbs tells us that "a merry heart makes a cheerful countenance, but by sorrow of the heart the spirit is broken" (15:13). Life is difficult for all of us and "full of trouble" (Job 14:1). When Jesus was on this earth, He promised, "In this world you will have tribulation" (John 16:33). This verse will likely not show up in our list of favorite Bible promises, but it is a promise that God intends to keep. Fortunately, Jesus also tells us that He has "overcome the world," so we can "be of good cheer."

Solomon states that cheerfulness is actually good medicine: "A merry heart does good, like medicine, but a broken spirit dries the bones" (Proverbs 17:22). Modern research confirms this ancient biblical wisdom. According to one researcher at the Johns Hopkins University School of Medicine, "A happier temperament has an actual effect on disease, and you may be healthier as a result."

In 2013, a study was published in the *American Journal of Cardiology* documenting 1,483 healthy people with siblings who had experienced some sort of coronary event (including heart attack and sudden cardiac death) before the age of 60. Even taking into account certain heart risk factors, it was found that having a positive wellbeing was linked with a one-third reduction in coronary events. Researchers also found that "among people who were most likely to experience a coronary event, having a positive wellbeing was linked with almost a 50 percent reduction in coronary events."[26]

We sometimes look at others from a distance and assume that everything is wonderful in their lives. We think it is only ourselves

---

[26] "Cheerful People Less Likely to Experience Heart Attacks, Study Suggests," The Huffington Post, July 11, 2103. http://www.huffingtonpost.com/2013/07/11/cheerful-heart-attack-risk-happy-well-being_n_3575548.html

who are struggling. However, the Bible teaches that everyone has troubles—no one is exempt. Jesus acknowledged this fact in the story of the wise and foolish builders (see Matthew 7:24-27). In this parable, one man built his house on solid rock and was saved, while the other built his house on the sand and perished. Notice that Jesus didn't say either man could avoid the storm—He just stated that the man who built on a strong foundation was saved.

We cannot always avoid the storm or choose the circumstances of our lives, but we can choose how we respond to life's challenges. In spite of everything, we *can* choose "in everything to give thanks; for this is the will of God in Christ Jesus" (1 Thessalonians 5:18). We can also choose with whom we will do life. Life is better when we wisely choose cheerful people.

Paul certainly chose friends who were cheerful. In his final letter, he spoke of a friend named Onesiphorus who was a continual source of encouragement to him. He wrote, "The Lord grant mercy to the household of Onesiphorus, for he often refreshed me, and was not ashamed of my chain" (2 Timothy 1:16). The word translated as "refreshed" in this verse was used to describe a cool fall breeze at the end of a miserably hot summer. Onesiphorus was a friend like that.

Paul was nearing the end of his life when he wrote this letter, and he was reflecting on the people who had made a difference. When you come to the end of your life, you will be thinking about the same. You will be thinking about the people who have meant the world to you. You will not be contemplating all the great toys and gadgets you bought at Best Buy or considering your accomplishments. You will be thinking about the people who encouraged you and cheered you on through the storms and trials in this world.

Keep Your Friends' Confidence

The story is told of three preachers who decided to go on a trip. As an exercise in honesty and transparency, they decided to share the biggest sin with which they struggled. The first preacher said his primary sin was lust. He struggled with looking at women inappropriately and even with pornography. The second preacher said he struggled with materialism. He saw people who had stuff and envied them. He never had enough. The third pastor shared that his number one sin was gossip, and he could not wait to get home and tell what he had learned!

Solomon tells us, "A talebearer reveals secrets, but he who is of a faithful spirit conceals a matter. . . A perverse man sows strife, and a whisperer separates the best of friends" (Proverbs 11:13; 16:28). I (Josh) know a man who always whispers when he gossips. He lowers his voice, looks around to see who might be able to hear, and then shares that juicy morsel. It would be better for him to keep it to himself. A whisperer separates close friends, but a wise friend keeps a confidence.

Be Candid in Your Friendships

When we are friends who keep confidences, others come to trust in us and know that we have their best interests at heart. This allows our friends to be candid with us about any shortcomings they see. In the same way, it allows us to be candid with them about their struggles and issues.

Solomon wrote, "Open rebuke is better than love carefully concealed" (Proverbs 27:5). Everyone has blind spots, and it can be an act of love to point out those spots to our friends—and for our friends to point them out in us. I sometimes wonder what everyone else knows about me that I don't know. I need people in my life who will be open with me, honest with me, and candid with me about those areas. I need friends who will speak the truth in love without judging me.

Sometimes we have to be bold and courageous enough to say the things that we don't want to say. Bill Hybels calls it "saying the last 10 percent." Most friends will tell us 90 percent of what we need to hear, but a true friend will tell us the last 10 percent. Pastor John Burke writes, "For most people, as soon as relationships get difficult, they bail out. They never let God lead them and grow them. But it is when things get difficult that God can teach us what love really does as we respond to Him."[27]

As we are being bold, we need to remember four rules for engaging in candid conversations. First, it is important to begin by examining our own hearts. Jesus said, "How can you say to your brother, 'Let me remove the speck from your eye'; and look, a plank is in your own eye? Hypocrite! First remove the plank from your own eye, and then you will see clearly to remove the speck from your brother's eye" (Matthew 7:4-5).

Second, we need to confront a friend in the right timing. Solomon writes, "A word spoken in due season, how good it is!" (Proverbs 15:23). We should correct our friends when they are up, not when they are down. Wise friends ask themselves, *Is this the appropriate time in this person's life for me to bring up the concern?*

---

[27] John Burke, *Soul Revolution: How Imperfect People Become All God Intended* (Grand Rapids, MI: Zondervan, 2008), p. 115.

Third, it is important for us to *compliment* our friends in public and *correct* them in private. This goes back to being kind—we never want to do something that would tear our friends down and humiliate them in front of others. There are exceptions to this rule. In Galatians 2:14, Paul wrote that he rebuked the disciple Peter "before them all." However, we have to remember that Peter committed the act publically, so Paul needed to rebuke it publically so the whole body could be corrected. The circle of correction needs to be about the same size as the circle of offense.

Finally, we should never rebuke others unless we are open to rebuke from them. The most difficult people to deal with are those who are quick to correct but are not open to receiving correction. As Solomon bluntly states, "Whoever loves instruction loves knowledge, but he who hates correction is stupid" (Proverbs 12:1).

Be Consistent in Your Relationships

To be wise in our friendships, we must be consistent in them. We can't allow ourselves to be fair-weather friends who are only around when things are going well. Rather, as Solomon states, we must be friends who love at all times and are born for adversity (see Proverbs 17:17). We are to be friends who stick "closer than a brother" (18:24b).

Humorist Erma Bombeck says, "A good friend is someone who thinks you are a good egg even though you are a little cracked." A good friend looks past any perceived imperfections in us and loves us anyway. We need people in our lives who will go through the mountains, valleys, and deserts with us. In the same way, we need to be a friend who will go through those same things with others. Wise friends are faithful, loyal, dependable, and trustworthy.

Billy Graham and Cliff Barrows demonstrated this type of friendship to each other's mutual benefit. The two met in 1945 shortly after Cliff and his wife, Billie, were on their honeymoon. The couple had scraped together just enough money to have a simple wedding and buy two train tickets to a resort town on the East Coast. However, when they arrived, they found that the hotel had been shut down.

The Barrows were stranded in an unfamiliar city with little money. Fortunately, a sympathetic driver took pity on them and drove them to a grocery store owned by a woman he knew. The newlyweds spent their first night in a room above the store. The woman arranged for them to spend the rest of their honeymoon at a friend's house, who in turn invited them to attend a local youth rally where a young evangelist was speaking.

Cliff and his wife attended the rally in Ashville, North Carolina. As it turned out, the song leader was sick that night, and Cliff was asked to take charge of the music. The "young evangelist" featured that night was, of course, Billy Graham, and the two become partners.[28] One of the keys to Billy Graham's success over the years can be traced back to friendships like these that he formed. He has surrounded himself with faithful, wise men like Cliff—friends that stick closer than a brother.

Get Wise!

"As iron sharpens iron, so a man sharpens the countenance of his friend" (Proverbs 27:17). Good friends can sharpen our rough edges and help us to be better spouses, parents, and servants of God. The key is in being discerning and choosing *wise* friends. Solomon

---

[28] Craig B. Larson, ed., *750 Engaging Illustrations* (Grand Rapids, MI: Baker Books, 2007).

writes, "The righteous should choose his friends carefully, for the way of the wicked leads them astray" (Proverbs 12:26).

So, where can you find these wise friends? One of the best places is in a small group at church. This is a place where godly people gather who know your name and your needs. It is not enough to just attend a worship service—you need to be in a small group where you can interact frequently and intimately with other believers. If you can't find a small group, consider starting one of your own. Gather some of your friends together at your church or into your home and simply study the Word of God together. You could go through a book like this one and discuss the key passages together.

Remember that the quality of your life is directly related to the quality of your relationships. So choose your friends wisely.

Wise Up About Conflict

In the last chapter, we discussed the importance of being both kind and candid in our relationships. Unfortunately, despite our best efforts, we will encounter conflicts in our interactions with friends and others. Try as we might to run from conflict, it will find us. If we don't know how to resolve these blow ups, we will suffer the consequences.

There is perhaps no greater illustration in American history of how *not* to handle conflict than the infamous family feud between the Hatfields and the McCoys. The trouble began in 1878 when Randolph McCoy (the leader of the McCoy family) accused his neighbor Floyd Hatfield of stealing a hog. The matter was taken to the local justice of the peace in Kentucky, who happened to be related to the Hatfields. Of course, the verdict went in favor of the Hatfields.

In retaliation, two McCoy brothers killed the lead witness in the case. Then, in 1881, the feud escalated when Roseanna McCoy entered into a relationship with Johnse Hatfield. In 1882, three McCoy family members killed Ellison Hatfield, which led Devil Anse Hatfield (the leader of the Hatfield family) to organize a lynch mob to seek revenge. All three McCoys were killed.

The feud reached its peak in 1888 when several members of the Hatfield family surrounded the cabin of Randolph McCoy and set it on fire. Randolph escaped, but two of his children were killed. The remaining McCoys moved to West Virginia, but the feud went on.

By 1891, it had claimed more than a dozen members on each side. At one point the Governor of West Virginia became so exasperated that he threatened to have his militia invade Kentucky.

Note that all this started with a disagreement about a *hog*. Clearly, retaliation and revenge are not wise ways to handle a problem. Yet this is how so many of us today deal with conflict. In truth, conflict can be one of the healthiest things for a relationship. It doesn't matter what the disagreement is about—even if it is over ownership of a pig—as long as the participants work out their differences in the right way. So, how do we wise up about conflict?

Control Your Tone

The first way to gain wisdom in managing conflict is to be aware of your tone of voice when a disagreement arises. Think of approaching a fire with a bucket of gasoline in one hand and a bucket of water in the other. If you pour gasoline on the fire, it will rise into an inferno. If you pour water on the fire, it will begin to die down. The same is true of your words. If you answer in a harsh tone, the conflict will escalate. But if you give a soft answer, the flames will begin to diminish. Solomon sums this up when he says, "A soft answer turns away wrath, but a harsh word stirs up anger" (Proverbs 15:1).

The tone of your voice has more to do with your success in dealing with conflict than any other factor. If you respond to another person in a sarcastic or snippy manner, he or she will perceive that tone in your voice and retaliate. Even if you are right, you and the other person will end up losing because feelings will be hurt, and you will cause damage to your relationship. You are never justified in using a snippy tone, no matter how much you try to rationalize to yourself that you are.

Research shows that parents who use a harsh tone with their teenagers have more problems with them. Their children are also more likely to experience depression than those from their softer-spoken counterparts. Shouting at your child will not improve his or her behavior.[29] What will make a difference are consequences. Not nagging or a harsh tone, but specific penalties you enforce for improper behavior.

Memorize Proverbs 15:1. Post it on your mirror. Make it your screen saver on your computer. Meditate on it as you go to sleep at night. It is without doubt the most powerful principle to consider when dealing with conflict, and you can apply it before, during, and after a disagreement arises.

Control Your Anger

Controlling your tone in a conflict is often a result of controlling your anger. Solomon states, "The beginning of strife is like releasing water; therefore stop contention before a quarrel starts" (Proverbs 17:14). According to research conducted by psychologist John Gottman, the way couples begin their conversations is an accurate predictor of the subsequent course of that conversation. If a person starts out being angry, the situation is almost certain to deteriorate and end badly.[30]

---

[29] Nancy Shute, "Parents' Harsh Words Might Make Teen Behaviors Worse," NPR, September 5, 2013. http://www.npr.org/blogs/health/2013/09/04/218972701/parents-harsh-words-might-make-teen-behaviors-worse
[30] Howard J. Markman, Scott M. Stanley, and Susan L. Blumberg, *Fighting for Your Marriage* (New York: John Wiley & Sons, 2010), p. 60.

I (Josh) like how Eugene Peterson phrases Proverbs 17:14: "The start of a quarrel is like a leak in a dam, so stop it before it bursts" (MSG). When I was a child, our family lived in the mountains of the Philippines, and I used to enjoy building little dams. Of course, the dams were not strong, and invariably the water would break over the top. Once it did, that small break would soon tear through the entire dam.

Anger is much like that. Once we start dialing it up, things tend to escalate quickly. Anger begets anger, when we express that anger, it comes right back to us. It's much like what happened in the Hatfield and McCoy feud, with one side dialing up the anger and the other side retaliating. The crazy cycle just continues to escalate.

If we want to be wise in handling conflict, we have to learn how to control our anger. Of course, this is not always easy, especially if the other person is clearly in the wrong. However, we have to remember that a furious person "abounds in transgression" (Proverbs 29:22). If our standard method of operation is to jump to rage when conflict arises, we will abound in transgression. What matters is not whether we are right but how we respond to the situation. As Solomon puts it, "A wrathful man stirs up strife, but he who is slow to anger allays contention" (Proverbs 15:18).

Notice that Solomon speaks of the person who is "slow to anger." That is exactly how God is described in passages such as Numbers 14:18: "The Lord is slow to anger and filled with unfailing love" (NLT). Jesus was slow to anger, but He did turn over some tables occasionally. He had a righteous anger when He saw the moneychangers defiling the Temple of God (see Matthew 21:12-17). Being slow to anger doesn't mean that there is never a time or place for it. However, it is the exception, not the rule.

Some people think they need to get their anger out. They imagine themselves as a pressure cooker, and if they don't release that pressure, they will explode. They wrongly believe that by expressing the anger it will somehow dissipate. However, the research shows that venting anger only makes it worse. Psychologist Carol Tavris notes, "Talking out an emotion doesn't reduce it, it rehearses it. People who are most prone to give vent to their rage get angrier, not less angry."[31]

If we want to be wise in handling conflict, we have to realize that the words we speak in anger can have lasting consequences. Later, when the argument is over, we might regret what we've said and want to take it back, but we will never be able to remove the hurt or the memory. Permanent damage has been done because we chose to enter the cycle of anger. The solution? Don't get into the cycle in the first place.

Seek Understanding

One way that we can curb our anger is to put ourselves in the other person's shoes and try to see things from his or her perspective. Anger springs up when we perceive that another person is trying to hurt us, but often that is not the other person's intention. When we choose to seek understanding before reacting, we take a significant step on the road to becoming wise. Several proverbs confirm this fact:

> In the multitude of words sin is not lacking, but he who restrains his lips is wise (Proverbs 10:19).

---

[31] Jane E. Brody, "Venting Anger May Do More Harm than Good," The New York Times, March 8, 1983. http://www.nytimes.com/1983/03/08/science/venting-anger-may-do-more-harm-than-good.html

Do you see a man hasty in his words? There is more hope for a fool than for him (Proverbs 29:20).

He who answers a matter before he hears it, it is folly and shame to him (Proverbs 18:13).

We have to engage our ears before we engage our mouths. If the other person doesn't feel heard and understood, there is nothing we can say to convince him or her of our position. Conversely, there is something deeply satisfying about being understood. So, how do we do this? One useful tool is known as "mirroring." This is where we respond in a way that communicates to the other person that we are seeking to gain understanding into how he or she feels. Some examples include:

- "You sound really frustrated."
- "Yes, that would have made me really mad."
- "So, what I hear you saying is . . ."

You will be surprised at how often you use that last line and the person says, "No, that is not what I am saying," or, "No, that is not quite right." The goal of mirroring is not to just repeat back what is being said but to *communicate* the emotion the other person is feeling.

You will find that it might take some time to get this right. You may be tempted to rush the process or convince yourself that you understand "well enough." However, as Steven Covey notes, "Empathic listening takes time, but it doesn't take anywhere near as much time as it takes to back up and correct misunderstandings when you're already miles down the road, to redo, to live with unexpressed and unsolved problems, to deal with the results of not giving people psychological air."[32]

So, before you enter into a conflict, watch your tone, control your anger, and seek to understand. That leads us to what to do when it is time to respond.

Admit Where You Are Wrong

In Proverbs 27:5-6, we read, "Open rebuke is better than love carefully concealed. Faithful are the wounds of a friend, but the kisses of an enemy are deceitful." According to the Bible, it is actually a *good* thing when someone rebukes us and points out our faults, for "he who covers his sins will not prosper, but whoever confesses and forsakes them will have mercy" (28:13). For this reason, we need to carefully consider the truth of the person's words and examine the areas where we may be wrong.

The key to dealing with conflict is an attitude of humility. If you are unable to admit *any* wrongdoing in the situation, there is a good chance that pride is an issue in your life. As Solomon notes, this has consequences: "By pride comes nothing but strife, but with the well-advised is wisdom" (13:10). Pride creates *strife*. You need to be willing to admit that you are wrong and admit that you are part of the problem. Then, as James states, you must "confess your trespasses to one another, and pray for one another, that you may be healed" (5:16).

Do you know someone who never admits he or she is wrong? Does that person have rich, deep, and satisfying relationships? I didn't

---

[32] Stephen R. Covey, *The 7 Habits of Highly Effective People* (New York, Simon & Schuster, 1989).

think so. People who are skilled at relationships are humble enough to admit when they are wrong. For this reason, dealing with conflict begins with awareness that you are part of the problem—and that you are willing to admit that to the other person.

Deal with One Issue at a Time

Solomon writes, "An ungodly man digs up evil, and it is on his lips like a burning fire. . . . He who covers a transgression seeks love, but he who repeats a matter separates friends" (Proverbs 16:27; 17:9). Ungodly people dig up evil. They may say they forgive an offense, but they will keep bringing it up.

It is much like the story of the man who said to his friend, "When my wife gets angry, she gets totally historical!" His friend looked puzzled. "Don't you mean *hysterical*?" he replied. "No," said the man. "She gets *historical*. She brings up everything I have ever done!"

Don't get historical. Just deal with the issue at hand. Jesus said, "If your brother sins against you, go and tell him his fault between you and him alone. If he hears you, you have gained your brother" (Matthew 18:15). Notice that the word "fault" is singular. One fault at a time. One issue at a time.

By "covering" another person's transgression, it doesn't mean we ignore or deny the issue. In any conflict, the goal is to discuss problems so that they can be resolved, and that doesn't happen by pretending they don't exist. Rather, "covering" means that we don't broadcast the matter to everyone or dig up past situations as evidence to support our position. We cover the other person's transgression and admit our own.

Fools make a big deal of other's faults and minimize their own. The wise openly admit their shortcomings and bear with the faults of others.

Attack Only the Problem

When it comes to conflict, some people's words can be like the piercings of the sword. Solomon refers to this in Proverbs 12:18 when he states, "There is one who speaks like the piercings of a sword, but the tongue of the wise promotes health." Fools attack the other person by belittling and name-calling, but the wise attack the problem.

Perhaps you can recall things that were said to you years ago in the midst of a heated conflict. Harmful words have a way of sticking with us. Like a sword, they can penetrate deep and leave a wound that is difficult to completely heal, which is why it is so important for you to choose your words carefully.

In Proverbs 29:11 we read, "A fool vents all his feelings, but a wise man holds them back." When you are in the midst of a conflict, know when to stop and don't allow anger or feelings of personal hurt to direct the conversation. Avoid sarcasm, insults, belittling statements, and exaggerations. These things won't solve the problem, and they can cause permanent damage to the relationship. Instead, focus on solving the issue so you can bring health and restoration to the friendship.

Decide to Forgive

Once the conflict is over, it important to take steps to forgive the other person for any wrong done. Solomon states, "Hatred stirs up strife, but love covers all sins" (Proverbs 10:12). To "cover" over sins means to forgive them. This is such an important concept that we find it repeated in the New Testament in places such as 1 Peter 4:8: "Above all things have fervent love one another, for 'love will cover a multitude of sins.'" Jesus said, "For if you forgive men their trespasses, your heavenly Father will also forgive you. But if you do not forgive men their trespasses, neither will your Father forgive your trespasses" (Matthew 6:14-15).

My (Steve) parents recently celebrated their sixty-fifth anniversary, and I asked my father to share what he had learned after all those years about what was the key to a lasting marriage. My dad is the quiet type and doesn't say much, but when he speaks we all listen because we know he has something wise to say. When I urged him to respond he said, "You have to forgive each other."

What ruins relationships? Why do marriages fall apart? The reason is not because of conflict. In fact, research from John Gottman shows that some of the happiest and longest-lasting relationships are those filled with conflict. Rather, the evidence shows that *bitterness* ends relationships—and bitterness is caused by the parties' unwillingness to forgive one another. As the old saying goes, "Bitterness is like drinking poison and waiting for the other person to die."

Solomon writes, "The discretion of a man makes him slow to anger, and his glory is to overlook a transgression" (Proverbs 19:11). The wise do not hold on to anger but choose to forgive the other person. Forgiveness roots out bitterness.

Come to a Resolution

Once bitterness has been displaced, it opens the door for resolution and restitution to occur. Solomon writes, "It is honorable for a man to stop striving, since any fool can start a quarrel" (Proverbs 20:3), and, "Better is a dry morsel with quietness, than a house full of feasting with strife" (17:1).

Any fool can start a quarrel, but wise people know how to stop one. They recognize that without forgiveness and resolution, they will only end up with a situation like the Hatfield and McCoy feud, with neither side being willing to budge. Wise people acknowledge that holding on to anger and bitterness has consequences—and that those consequences affect not only the other person but also themselves.

Get Wise!

You will experience conflict in this life, so it's important for you to learn how to handle it in a way that won't lead to bitterness and pain. Be aware of how you enter into a conflict (watch your tone and control your anger), and then go through the steps outlined in this chapter. Always forgive the person, and work to find a solution. Finally, consider this important rule of thumb: Do not ever have the same fight twice. Don't be back at the same place the next week. Move on and find something new to fight about!

Remember that the quality of your relationships has much to do with how wisely you choose to handle conflicts with others. So be wise when you fight.

Wise Up About Sex

William Jefferson Clinton was re-elected to a second term as President of the United States with one of the highest approval ratings in modern times. At one point, he had a Gallup Poll rating of 66 percent—the highest of any president since World War II. Yet he almost lost it all in 1998 when news of an affair between him and Monica Lewinsky, a White House intern, was leaked to the press.

News of the scandal first broke on January 17, 1998. Despite denials from Clinton, the allegations would not go away. By August 17, Clinton had to admit to a grand jury that he had engaged in an "improper physical relationship" with Lewinsky. His admission led to impeachment hearings in December on the basis of perjury and obstruction of justice. Although he was ultimately acquitted, the affair tarnished his legacy and left a lasting impression on the public's mind. Upon leaving office, 68 percent of the population believed that he would be most remembered for his involvement in the scandal, while 58 percent believed he was dishonest and untrustworthy.[33]

Clinton is not alone. Many other famous celebrities have been found lacking wisdom in the area of sex. For some, the damage to their lives and career has been severe, just as it was for Clinton. While sex can be an enormous blessing through the pleasure, closeness, and intimacy it brings to a couple, it can also cause unspeakable pain. As

---

[33] Keating Holland, "Poll: Majority of Americans Glad Clinton Is Leaving Office," CNN, January 10, 2001.

a pastor, I have listened to hundreds of people pour out their tears because a sexual relationship broke their hearts.

Regardless of what your standard is for sexuality—and everyone has *some* standard—you will be tempted. If you hold to the biblical standard, you will be tempted to break God's commandments. If you hold to some other standard, you will be tempted to violate those standards. No one is exempt—politicians, businessmen, law enforcement officials, athletes, Christians, and even pastors will all be tempted.

In Proverbs, Solomon deals with most of the topics in a somewhat random way. For instance, if you want to find all the proverbs about money, communication, or relationships, you pretty much have to read the whole book. Sex is the exception. Apparently, the topic of sex was so important to Solomon that he decided to give it concentrated and focused attention.

There are several long sections in Proverbs that deal with sex (Proverbs 2:16-22; 6:24-35; 7:5-27; 9:13-18), but in this chapter we will focus our attention on Proverbs 5:1-23. We will begin by looking at the context of the passage (and how we are to teach this information to our children) and then examine the main message of the chapter. This can be reduced to two major points: (1) say no to sex outside of marriage, and (2) say yes to sex inside of marriage.

Teach Your Children About Immorality

Solomon begins this passage on sexual morality with these words: "My son, pay attention to my wisdom; lend your ear to my understanding" (Proverbs 5:1). Notice that the context is that of a father advising his son on this oh-so-delicate topic. Some of us parents feel awkward discussing sex with our children, so we avoid the subject. Some of us allow public school or the culture to educate our kids. However, the biblical way is that we as parents counsel our own children about sex.

We need to take this responsibility seriously. We must have "the talk" with our kids. I (Steve) remember when my mother had "the talk" with me. One day she said, "Come over here." When I came over, I saw that she had this book with all kinds of pictures in it. (My father was nowhere to be found.) We talked about the pictures and what was in that book, and part of our discussion was about morality. My mom talked about her life and the mistakes she had made. She was honest, clear, and real.

Was this uncomfortable for me? Yes. Was it weird? Yes. Was it life changing? Yes. I tried to act cool, but I was hanging on her every word. I wanted to hear what my mom had to say, and I am so grateful that she had the courage to tackle such a tough subject. I believe that God helped me not to make the same mistakes my mom had made partly because she had the courage to have "the talk."

If you are at a loss of what to say with your kids, go through Proverbs 5. Use the following material in this chapter as a guide to help you talk about what is right and what is wrong. Explain that God created sex as a *gift* to men and women. Sex is not dirty but is beautiful when it takes place between a man and wife.

Say No to Sex Outside of Marriage

The Bible emphatically condemns premarital and extramarital sex. Paul said, "For this is the will of God, your sanctification: that you should abstain from sexual immorality; that each of you should know how to possess his own vessel in sanctification and honor" (1 Thessalonians 4:3-4). God's will is for us to be *sanctified,* which means holy. Jesus said it this way: "Therefore you shall be perfect, just as your Father in heaven is perfect" (Matthew 5:48).

You might object and say that because no one can truly be perfect, why should we set our sights on it? Isn't God just setting us up for a fall? Author Jerry Bridges offers this answer: "Can you imagine a soldier going into battle with the aim of 'not getting hit very much'? The very suggestion is ridiculous. His aim is not to get hit at all! Yet if we have not made a commitment to holiness without exception, we are like a soldier going into battle with the aim of not getting hit very much. We can be sure if that is our aim, we will be hit—not with bullets, but with temptation over and over again."[34]

God's standard for holiness in sex is simple: it is to be between a husband and wife. Not between a man and a woman who are not married, nor between a man and a man, nor between a woman and a woman. Paul writes, "God gave them [the ungodly] up to vile passions. For even their women exchanged the natural use for what is against nature. Likewise also the men, leaving the natural use of the woman, burned in their lust for one another, men with men committing what is shameful, and receiving in themselves the penalty of their error which was due" (Romans 1:26-27). God's Word calls acts of homosexuality *vile* and *unnatural.* God considers anything outside of sex between a husband and his wife to be immorality.

---

[34] Jerry Bridges, *The Pursuit of Holiness* (Colorado Springs, CO: Navpress, 1978), p. 93.

In 1 Thessalonians 4:4, Paul adds, "Each of you should know how to possess his own vessel in sanctification and honor." It is not enough for us to simply *resolve* to say no to sex outside of marriage. We must *know* how to keep God's standard, and this involves being able to recognize temptation when it comes. The wisdom in Proverbs can help us identify how the enemy will attack us in this area.

Recognize Temptation

The first step in avoiding sexual immorality is to recognize temptation when it comes. Solomon writes, "The lips of an immoral woman drip honey, and her mouth is smoother than oil; but in the end she is bitter as wormwood" (Proverbs 5:3-4). The "immoral woman" in this sense represents temptation, which looks good on the surface but only leads to ruin. "Her feet go down to death, her steps lay hold of hell" (verse 5).

If Solomon were writing today, he might say, "Listen, son, there will be lots of temptations out there—lots of readily available pornography and women who 'just want to have a good time.' You are going to have to deal with these temptations in the midst of a society that does not accept God's standard for sexuality. Just remember that God is good, and following Him is good. It will always be in your best interest to live the Christian life. God's plan for your life, in terms of your sexuality, is good for you in the long run, but in the short run you will be tempted to veer from it."

Paul, writing to a church that had a big problem in this area, said, "The body is not for sexual immorality but for the Lord, and the Lord for the body. . . . Do you not know that your bodies are members of Christ? Shall I then take the members of Christ and make them members of a harlot? Certainly not! Or do you not know that he who is joined to a harlot is one body with her? For 'the two,' He says, 'shall become one flesh.' But he who is joined to the Lord is one spirit with Him. Flee sexual immorality. Every sin that a man does is outside the body, but he who commits sexual immorality sins against his own body" (1 Corinthians 6:13,15-16-18).

Notice both the negative and the positive in Paul's words. The purpose of your body is not for sexual immorality but for the Lord. God created your body for a purpose, and that purpose is not sexual immorality. Furthermore, as a Christian, the Holy Spirit inhabits (or indwells) your body. This means that everywhere you go, you take the Holy Spirit with you. Whatever you do, the Holy Spirit is there. If you go to bed with someone who is not your spouse, you are taking the Holy Spirit with you.

Jesus said, "For there is nothing covered that will not be revealed, nor hidden that will not be known" (Luke 12:2). God is watching. What is done in secret is not a secret to Him. He sees every look, every act, and every flirtatious hint. He hates the effects of sin, because He knows the pain that is coming.

Don't Be Taken in By Lies

The second step in maintaining sexual purity is to not be taken in by the enemy's lies. One popular lie circulating today is that it makes sense for a couple to "test drive" a marriage by living with each other first. Since 1960, cohabitation in the United States has jumped from approximately 450,000 unmarried couples to more than 7.5 million. Today, the majority of adults in their twenties will live with at least one partner, and more than 50 percent of married couples will have first lived together.[35]

However, the research shows that cohabitation does not lead to better marriages. According to a recent survey conducted by the National Marriage Project, "Couples who cohabit before marriage (and especially before an engagement or an otherwise clear commitment) tend to be less satisfied with their marriages—and more likely to divorce—than couples who do not."[36]

Research also shows that promiscuous teenagers are not as happy as they pretend to be. A study commissioned by MTV and the Associated Press found that girls who are highly promiscuous tended to be more depressed and suicidal than their less promiscuous counterparts. Furthermore, "Nearly three-quarters of people between the ages of 13 and 24 said their relationship with their parents makes them happy. They also said having sex and using drugs doesn't really make them happy and spirituality is important to them."[37] As Philip Yancey sums up, "Teenagers worry that they will miss out on something if they heed the Bible's warnings against premarital sex. Actually, the warnings are there to keep them from missing out on something."[38]

The belief that sex outside of marriage leads to greater happiness and fulfillment is nothing but a lie from the enemy. Jesus said of him, "He was a murderer from the beginning, and does not stand

---

[35] Meg Jay, "The Downside of Cohabiting Before Marriage," The New York Times, April 14, 2012. http://www.nytimes.com/2012/04/15/opinion/sunday/the-downside-of-cohabiting-before-marriage.html?pagewanted=all&_r=0

[36] Ibid.

[37] Erin Roach, "Family Makes Teens Happiest, Study Finds," Baptist Press, August 31, 2007. http://www.bpnews.net/bpnews.asp?ID=26360

[38] Philip Yancey, Rumors of Another World (Grand Rapids, MI: Zondervan, 2003).

in the truth, because there is no truth in him. When he speaks a lie, he speaks from his own resources, for he is a liar and the father of it" (John 8:44). The truth, as the research clearly shows, is that "the happiest couples are the monogamous couples."[39] So be wise, and don't fall for the enemy's lies.

Stay Away from Temptation

Sex outside of marriage causes unspeakable heartache, yet people fall into temptation every day. Typically, the reason for this is because they fail to stay away from sexual temptation and think through all the consequences of their actions. So, how can you avoid falling into the same trap?

The first step is to simply and humbly admit that you are susceptible to sexual immorality. Whether you are single or married, you are never above sexual temptation. Paul wrote, "Let him who thinks he stands take heed lest he fall" (1 Corinthians 10:12). The enemy likes to prey on our pride, and we need to be alert that "pride goes before destruction, and a haughty spirit before a fall" (Proverbs 16:18).

Once you acknowledge that you are *vulnerable* to sexual sin, it puts you in a better place to stay away from temptation. Solomon wrote, "Remove your way far from her [sexual temptation], and do not go near the door of her house" (Proverbs 5:8). Notice that last line: "Do not go near." Andy Stanley explains how he does this: "I don't go to lunch with a woman. I don't ride in a car alone with a woman. I don't counsel a woman alone. I don't meet with a woman alone. I don't talk to a woman about anything personal. I am never alone

---

[39] Garrison Keillor, "It's Good Old Monogamy That's Really Sexy," TIME, October 17, 1994. http://www.time.com/time/magazine/article/0,9171,981618-1,00.html#ixz-z0I5SPQuwZ

with another woman for any reason." Truly wise people don't put themselves in situations where it is easy for the enemy to tempt them to sin.

A final way to stay clear of temptation is to seriously think through the consequences of your sin *before* you act. Satan, the father of lies, will attempt to magnify the pleasure of sin and minimize its cost, so you would do well to do the opposite: magnify the cost of sin and think soberly about the fact that its pleasure is only for a season. Consider some of the things that Solomon says comes about as a result of sexual immorality:

> Remove your way far from her . . . lest you give your honor to others, and your years to the cruel one; lest aliens be filled with your wealth, and your labors go to the house of a foreigner; and you mourn at last, when your flesh and your body are consumed, and say: "How I have hated instruction, and my heart despised correction! I have not obeyed the voice of my teachers, nor inclined my ear to those who instructed me! I was on the verge of total ruin, in the midst of the assembly and congregation" (Proverbs 5:8-14).

Remember that there are no victimless sins. Sin hurts everyone, and sexual sin will damage the relationships you have with those you love the most. It will also affect your relationship with God. Keep Job's words in mind: "I have made a covenant with my eyes; why then should I look upon a young woman?" (Job 31:1).

Say Yes to Sex Inside Marriage

The Bible is clear that we should avoid sex *outside* of marriage, but it is equally clear that we should enjoy it *inside* of marriage. God created sex, and everything that God creates is good. Sex in marriage is actually honorable to God.

Solomon points to this fact when he advises, "Drink water from your own cistern, and running water from your own well. Should your fountains be dispersed abroad, streams of water in the streets? Let them be only your own, and not for strangers with you" (Proverbs 5:15-17). In Solomon's day, water was so precious and scarce that to take it from another was to take the source of his or her life. This reveals the immense value that God places on sex inside of marriage. We must drink from our own "cistern" and not be with someone who is not our spouse.

Solomon concludes by stating, "Let your fountain be blessed, and rejoice with the wife of your youth. As a loving deer and a graceful doe, let her breasts satisfy you at all times; and always be enraptured with her love" (verses 18-19). This is a passage you don't often hear in church! Yet it once again affirms the fact that sex is not dirty and that its purpose is not just for reproduction. The Song of Solomon, another book in the Bible by Solomon, is primarily about the pleasures of sex.

Sex inside of marriage creates a strong bond between a man and a woman and will help those in the relationship resist temptation. In the same way that we won't be tempted to buy as much food at the grocery store when we have a full stomach, we won't be as tempted to sin sexually when we are satisfied at home. As Paul advises, "Do not deprive one another except with consent for a time, that you may give yourselves to fasting and prayer; and come together again so that Satan does not tempt you because of your lack of self-control" (1 Corinthians 7:5).

Of course, there is a minority of believers who are gifted with singleness, and for them the Bible teaches that it is better to be single. Paul was one such individual, and he said, "I wish that all men were even as I myself. But each one has his own gift from God, one in this manner and another in that" (verse 7). However, for the rest of us, it is God's plan that we be married and enjoy the incredible gift of sex that He has given to us.

Get Wise!

Temptations come in all forms, and few are as powerful (especially for men) as the temptation of sexual immorality. The key to wisdom in this area is to recognize that you are vulnerable, take steps to avoid temptation, and carefully consider the consequences. To this end, I close with this partial list from Charles Swindoll of what you have to look forward to if you commit sexual immorality and are found out:

- Your mate will experience betrayal, shame, rejection, heartache, and loneliness. No amount of repentance will soften those blows.

- Your mate can never again say that you are a model of fidelity. Suspicion will rob her or him of trust.

- Your escapades will introduce to your life and your mate's life the very real probability of a sexually transmitted disease.

- Your children's growth, innocence, trust, and healthy outlook on life will be severely and permanently damaged.

- You will cause indescribable heartache to your parents, your family, and your peers.

- You will have to face the disappointment of other Christians who once appreciated you, respected you, and trusted you.

- If you are engaged in the Lord's work, you will suffer immediate loss of your job and the support of those with whom you worked. The dark shadow will accompany you everywhere . . . and forever.

- Your fall will give others license to do the same.

- The inner peace you enjoyed will be gone.

- You will never be able to erase the fall from your (or others') mind. It will remain indelibly etched on your life's record regardless of your later return to your senses.

- The name of Jesus Christ, whom you once honored, will be tarnished, giving the enemies of the faith further reason to sneer and jeer. [40]

Don't be a fool when it comes to sexual morality. Be faithful to God and to your spouse. Submit to God. "Resist the devil [and his temptations], and he will flee from you" (James 4:7). Wise up and live a long and happy life.

---

[40] Chuck Swindoll, *Swindoll's Ultimate Book of Illustrations and Quotes* (Nashville, TN: Thomas Nelson, 2003).

Wise Up About Addictions

The story is told of a man who took a business trip to Southeast Asia and came across a baby elephant lying in the road. The man thought it would be fun to own such a creature, so he arranged to have it brought back to America. However, he was concerned about what his family and friends would say, so he decided to disguise it as a table. He put the little elephant in his living room, draped a cloth over it, and pretended that everything was perfectly normal.

The man's family was concerned about this new addition to their household, but he seemed defensive when they asked him about it, so they decided not to confront him. Some in the family figured it was an innocent diversion, while others thought the problem would go away on its own if they ignored it. So, day after day they said nothing and just cleaned up the mess that the creature would leave in their living room.

The man fed table scraps to the little elephant, and before long it wasn't such a little elephant anymore. Soon, the man found that he was putting out quite a bit of cash every week to keep the animal. The creature was causing bigger and bigger messes that the family continued to clean up, and it was now so large that it was damaging the furniture and starting to crush the floorboards. Before long, the tablecloth the man had used barely covered the animal. Everyone was finding it harder and harder to hide the fact that there was an elephant in room.

Addictions—those sins we find hard to refuse—are a lot like owning a little elephant. At first they seem innocent and fun diversions, but over time they turn into strongholds that damage lives and destroy relationships. The family member of an addict might try to cover up the problem, pretend it doesn't exist, or think if they do nothing it will go away, but as time goes on things will only get worse. Addictions will grow until they are no longer possible to hide, at which point the addict will seek help or succumb to the consequences of his or her chosen behavior.

Wise people don't allow the addiction into their house, and they certainly don't feed it and allow it to grow. They also do not ignore the problem when someone else is suffering from an addiction. So, how can you be wise in this area?

Recognize the Source of Addiction

The first step is to understand that almost *anything* in this world can be source of addiction. While most of us recognize that alcohol, drugs, smoking, gambling, and pornography can be addictive, we can also get bound to money, work, food, laziness, shopping, or even Facebook. In 2 Corinthians 10:5, Paul calls these "strongholds."

Jesus said that the greatest command is this: "Love the LORD your God with all your heart, with all your soul, and with all your mind" (Matthew 22:37). Notice the phrase "with all your heart." Loving anything more than we love God is sin. Counselor Ed Welch says, "An addiction is a worship disorder. Instead of worshiping the divine King, addicts worship idols that temporarily satisfy physical desire."[41] In Ezekiel 14:3, God states, "Son of man, these men have set up their

---

[41] Edward T. Welch, *Addictions: A Banquet in a Grave* (Phillipsburg, NJ: P&R Publishing, 2001).

idols in their hearts." Idolatry is an issue of the heart. It is putting anything else before God.

Jesus taught that the enemy "does not come except to steal, and to kill, and to destroy" (John 10:10). To accomplish this goal, he will usually come to us with a temptation and try to get us to compromise our righteousness. "Just a little won't hurt," he will lie. "No one will ever know. Let's call it an *experiment*. It will satisfy your curiosity." If he can get us to succumb to the temptation, he will work to develop it into a stronghold, and soon the small addiction turns into a life-dominating sin.

Satan is a master at changing his strategies. He might first try to get us addicted to alcohol, but if that doesn't work, he will switch to porn. If that doesn't work, he might try to get us addicted to work, shopping, sugar, or sports—anything that will keep us from experiencing the abundant life that Jesus has promised.

It only takes one moment of weakness to ruin a life. I (Josh) once heard a story of a churchgoing Christian whose car broke down on the freeway. The man who gave him a ride offered him some drugs, and though the Christian had never thought about consuming illegal substances before, his curiosity got the best of him. In a moment of weakness he took the drugs, got hooked, and ruined his life.

If we want to be wise, we can't fall for the enemy's trap. We need to recognize when Satan is trying to tempt us and be wary of his schemes. We need to stand strong and not allow Satan to convince us that it is a minor thing to sin against God.

Alcohol Addiction

Addictions come in all shapes and sizes, but let's look at two in particular that are addressed in the book of Proverbs, beginning with alcohol. In Proverbs 23:29-31, we read, "Who has woe? Who has sorrow? Who has contentions? Who has complaints? Who has wounds without cause? Who has redness of eyes? Those who linger long at the wine, those who go in search of mixed wine. Do not look on the wine when it is red, when it sparkles in the cup, when it swirls around smoothly."

Notice that last part about not looking on the wine when it "sparkles" in the cup. This can be applied to nearly every area of life. Satan will find a way to make the poison taste good. He will find ways to make what destroys us seem attractive, just as he did with Eve in the Garden of Eden. Remember that it was after he told Eve that the forbidden fruit would make her wise that she "saw that the tree was good for food, that it was pleasant to the eyes" (Genesis 3:6). Satan will make the wine sparkle in the cup.

However, in the end, the wine "bites like a serpent, and stings like a viper." If you become addicted to it, "Your eyes will see strange things, and your heart will utter perverse things. Yes, you will be like one who lies down in the midst of the sea, or like one who lies at the top of the mast, saying: 'They have struck me, but I was not hurt; they have beaten me, but I did not feel it'" (Proverbs 23:32-35). To a teenager, going to parties and getting drunk seems like a cool thing to do. But if you talk to a 45-year-old alcoholic, you get a much different picture. Ruined career. Ruined marriage. Ruined health. Ruined life. Jesus wants to save us from that path of destruction.

So, how do we know if alcohol has become a stronghold in our lives? Look at the words at the end of verse 35: "When shall I awake, that I may seek another drink?" No matter how much pain people who are addicted to alcohol experience, they always keep coming back for more. They lose their job, but they keep on drinking. They lose their marriage, but they keep on drinking. They suffer liver disease and other health issues, but they keep on drinking.

Solomon writes, "Wine is a mocker, strong drink is a brawler, and whoever is led astray by it is not wise" (Proverbs 20:1). When alcohol has the control, it has become a stronghold in our lives. When consequences no longer shape behavior, we can be certain that we are addicted to it.

Food Addiction

A second addiction that is addressed in the book of Proverbs is overeating. What is interesting about this addiction is that it does not carry the same negative associations that other addictions do. Every week, you can find preachers with their bellies flopped over the pulpit speaking about the sin of drugs and alcohol. They have gravy dripping down their chin the whole time they are screaming and hollering and pounding the pulpit about these other addictions. I (Steve) once knew a preacher like that—me.

Gluttony has become, in the words of Jerry Bridges, a "respectable sin."[42] We celebrate it at every potluck dinner. We see no shame in overeating at a buffet. And what is a good small group without Krispy Kreme donuts? God has a different take on the matter. In Proverbs we read, "When you sit down to eat with a ruler, consider carefully what is before you; and put a knife to your throat if you are a man given to appetite. Do not desire his delicacies, for they are deceptive food. . . . Do not mix with winebibbers, or with gluttonous eaters of meat" (Proverbs 23:1-3, 20).

---

[42] Jerry Bridges, *Respectable Sins* (Colorado Springs, CO: NavPress, 2007).

For me, verse 2 was convicting and life-changing: "put a knife to your throat if you are a man given to appetite." Even though I was more than 100 pounds overweight, I still ended each day with a bowl of ice cream. I lived that way for years, and because of my weight—and only because of my weight—I suffered from high blood pressure, high cholesterol, and diabetes. I'm not alone. A 2006 study conducted by Purdue University found that Christians are by far the heaviest of all religious groups, with Baptists leading the way at a 30 percent obesity rate. Compare this to the obesity rates of Jews at 1 percent and Buddhists and Hindus at .7 percent.[43]

Similarly, a 2011 study conducted by Northwestern University that tracked 3,433 men and women for 18 years found that young adults who attended church or a Bible study once a week were *50 percent* more likely to be obese.[44] In 2001, a study by Pulpit and Pew of 2,500 clergy revealed that 76 percent of pastors were overweight or obese, as compared to 61 percent of the general population at the time.[45]

The consequences of overeating can lead to health risks, just as with other addictions such as drugs and alcohol. According the Centers for Disease Control, as a person's weight increases to reach levels referred to as "overweight" (BMI 25–30) and "obese" (BMI 30+), the risk increases for that person to suffer from coronary heart disease, type 2 diabetes, endometrial cancer, breast cancer, colon cancer, hypertension (high blood pressure), dyslipidemia (high total cholesterol or high levels of triglycerides), stroke, liver disease, gallbladder disease, sleep apnea, respiratory problems, osteoarthritis (a degeneration of cartilage and its underlying bone

[43] Scott Stoll, MD, "Fat in Church," FOX News, January 4, 2013. http://www.foxnews.com/opinion/2012/06/03/obesity-epidemic-in-america-churches/
[44] Ibid.
[45] Ibid.

within a joint), and gynecological problems (such as abnormal menses and infertility).[46]

More and more today, we are not suffering health problems due to communicable diseases but due to our lifestyle choices. We are like a person who bangs his head with a hammer and then asks the doctor to give him more aspirin. We are eating ourselves into our graves. Overeating is as deadly and addicting as alcohol, which is why the Bible instructs us to take action against it. While the instruction in Proverbs 23:2 to "put a knife" to our throat is a hyperbole for sure, it serves as a strong warning for us to do something. It reminds me of Jesus' words in Matthew 5:29-30:

> If your right eye causes you to sin, pluck it out and cast it from you; for it is more profitable for you that one of your members perish, than for your whole body to be cast into hell. And if your right hand causes you to sin, cut it off and cast it from you; for it is more profitable for you that one of your members perish, than for your whole body to be cast into hell.

The message is clear: we must take whatever measures are necessary to rid ourselves of food addiction. It will kill us, so we can't take it lightly. When I came to this realization and surrendered my fork to God, it forever changed my life. I got rid of all three diseases, and I began to teach others about the dangers of this addiction.

As stated previously, food and alcohol are just two examples of addictions—there are countless others. However, regardless of what form the addiction takes, we all need to understand what is the underlying cause. The book of Proverbs has wisdom to share with us on this matter as well.

---

[46] "What Causes Overweight and Obesity," Centers for Disease Control, April 27, 2102. http://www.cdc.gov/obesity/adult/causes/index.html

Understand the Cause

In Proverbs 23:19, we read, "Hear, my son, and be wise; and guide your heart in the way." Notice the word "heart." Too many times we deal with symptoms of addiction instead of the true source of the disease. We have a Krispy Kreme donut in our hand and think that is the problem. We have alcohol in the cupboard and think that is the source. We click our mouse over a porn site and think that is the issue. The real problem is never what is on the outside but what is inside our heart.

In Jeremiah 17:9, the prophet states, "The human heart is the most deceitful of all things, and desperately wicked. Who really knows how bad it is?" (NLT). The human heart is deceitful, and the enemy will use it to convince us to engage in sin. We see this again in the story of Adam and Eve in the Garden of Eden. When Eve told the serpent that God had said they would die if they ate from the tree of the knowledge of good and evil, the enemy replied, "You will not surely die. For God knows that in the day you eat of it your eyes will be opened, and you will be like God" (Genesis 3:4-5). Satan knew that Eve found the fruit "pleasant to the eyes" and "desirable to make one wise" (verse 6), and he used what was in her heart to convince her to disobey God.

Notice that Jeremiah says the heart is not only deceitful but also *wicked*. We are not basically good—in fact, we are altogether bad. We are sinners, and it is in our nature to sin. David recognized this problem of the heart when he wrote, "Behold, I was brought forth in iniquity, and in sin my mother conceived me" (Psalm 51:5). Paul summed it up this way: "All have sinned and fall short of the glory of God" (Romans 3:23).

If you ever find yourself asking why you did such something that you know to be wrong, realize that it is because you are a sinner. *All have sinned*—that means all of us. So don't say, "I can't believe I did that!" Believe it. You did it because you are a sinner, and that's what sinners do. Your task is to accept that and acknowledge that you have a problem. Only then can you move down the path to recovery.

Guard Your Heart

When God told Samuel to anoint a new king over Israel, he sent him to the home of a man named Jesse, who had many sons. When Samuel looked at Eliab, the oldest boy, he said, "Surely the LORD's anointed is before Him!" But God said, "Do not look at his appearance or at his physical stature, because I have refused him. For the LORD does not see as man sees . . . the LORD looks at the heart" (1 Samuel 16:6-7).

God knows that the heart is the source of the problem, so His solution is always first and foremost a heart solution. This is why Solomon advises, "Keep your heart with all diligence, for out of it spring the issues of life" (Proverbs 4:23). Notice the phrase, "with all diligence." This tells us that keeping our hearts in the right place involves work. Just as our physical hearts beat constantly over 100,000 times a day, so we must be constant in the way we guard our hearts.

If you are a Christian, the first step you took toward guarding your heart occurred at salvation. Paul wrote, "If you confess with your mouth the Lord Jesus and believe in your heart that God has raised Him from the dead, you will be saved" (Romans 10:9). Note the first two words in this verse: "if you." God did not kick down the door of your heart. Jesus came "to seek and to save that which was lost" (Luke 19:10), but the choice was up to you. Because you chose to open the door, He gladly came into your life and began to transform you (see Revelation 3:20).

So, the process of guarding your heart has already begun. However, this is just the beginning, not the end. God doesn't want you to stay in that initial state—He wants you to grow in Christ-likeness. As Paul writes, God wants us to be mature in our faith so that "we should no longer be children, tossed to and fro and carried about with every wind of doctrine, by the trickery of men, in the cunning craftiness of deceitful plotting, but . . . grow up in all things into Him who is the head" (Ephesians 4:14-15).

When you have Christ in your heart, you can draw on His strength. I (Josh) remember a man I talked to more than twenty years ago about becoming a Christian. He gladly asked Christ to forgive him of his sins and become the Lord of his life. As he left, I emphasized that his decision wouldn't make all of his problems and temptations go away. He replied, "Yes, I understand that, but I won't have to go it alone." That can be true of you as well. You will still have to deal with addictions, but you will never have to deal with them alone.

Of course, salvation is not just about asking God to forgive our past sins. It also involves confessing our sins to God when we commit them in the present. It involves asking God to search us and correct us in His ways, as David writes: "Search me, O God, and know my heart; try me, and know my anxieties; and see if there is any wicked way in me, and lead me in the way everlasting" (Psalm 139:23). Confession and repentance are thus another way in which we guard our hearts.

In Ezekiel 14:6, God tells the people, "Repent, turn away from your idols, and turn your faces away from all your abominations." When some people see the word "repent," they immediately think it implies that they are bad. However, as this passage shows, what it actually means is to "turn away" and go in a different direction. If you are heading toward a life of ruin, you make a U-Turn and head toward a life of abundance. If you are heading toward a life in which God is on the sidelines, you make a U-Turn a start putting Him in first place.

You will never get the victory until you deal with the root cause. Just dealing with symptoms won't help. The root cause is a heart issue. So put God first in your heart.

Say Goodbye to the Wrong Friends

As we have already discussed in chapter 3, each of us can be drawn into sin through social pressure. This is why it is so important for us to make wise friends who will influence us to pursue the things of God and not of this world. Solomon comments on this frequently in Proverbs:

> Do not walk in the way with sinners who try to entice you, keep your foot from their path (1:15).

> The righteous should choose his friends carefully, for the way of the wicked leads them astray (12:26).

> He who walks with wise men will be wise, but the companion of fools will be destroyed (13:20).

> Make no friendship with an angry man, and with a furious man do not go, lest you learn his ways and set a snare for your soul (22:24-25).

In the New Testament, Paul sums it up this way: "Do not be deceived: 'Evil company corrupts good habits'" (1 Corinthians 15:33). The people who are in the inner circles of our lives have a profound influence on us. I (Josh) certainly witnessed this in my own life. I smoked my first cigarette because some friends talked me into it. The first time I ever saw pornography was because some friends convinced me to go to an X-rated movie. I drank alcohol for the first time because some of my friends around me were doing it. This is typically how addiction starts.

One of the most important decisions I (Steve) ever made was back when I was a senior in high school. I had been hanging out with some friends who were not leading me to the place I wanted to go, and I knew I needed to do something about it. So, I decided to walk away from those people—some of whom had been lifelong friends. It wasn't an easy choice to make, and I went through a time of loneliness where I didn't have any friends. However, God eventually brought some great people into my life, and my life has taken a different course because of it. Yet there was a time when I really struggled.

If you want to break an addiction, you might likewise have to walk away from some friends whom you've known all your life. They won't understand. They will be critical of you. There is no doubt that it will be hard and you will be lonely for a time. However, it will be necessary for you to do in order to break that addiction, and you can be assured that it will be worth it in the end.

Your companions will determine your character and your destiny in this life. So say goodbye to any friends who are not supporting you in godliness and choose wise friends who share your goals. After all, as we discussed in chapter 3, it will be easier for you to accomplish a goal if you have friends who are moving toward that same goal. As Solomon writes, "Two are better than one, because they have a good reward for their labor. For if they fall, one will lift up his companion" (Ecclesiastes 4:9-10).

Evaluate the Consequences

In Proverbs 7, Solomon relates the sad tale of a foolish man who yielded to temptation: "Immediately he went after her, as an ox goes to the slaughter or as a fool to the correction of the stocks, till an arrow struck his liver. As a bird hastens to the snare, he did not know it would cost his life" (verses 22-23). Addictions promise pleasure but only deliver pain. In the end, they rob us of the blessings and abundant life that Jesus wants us to have (see John 10:10).

Paul said, "All things are lawful for me, but all things are not helpful. All things are lawful for me, but I will not be brought under the power of any" (1 Corinthians 6:12). This is what addictions do—they bring us under the power of their control. Thus, as part of becoming wise in this area, we need to recognize that when we submit to temptation, we give the enemy access and control in our lives.

Solomon states that those who do not weigh the consequences of their actions "shall eat the fruit of their own way, and be filled to the full with their own fancies" (Proverbs 1:31). The apostle Paul makes the same point when he states, "Do not be deceived, God is not mocked; for whatever a man sows, that he will also reap" (Galatians 6:7). Behaviors have consequences. What we plant will grow.

Part of the genius of the 12-step model in programs such Alcoholics Anonymous is that they get addicts in touch with the consequences of their behaviors. Step 8 in most of these models requires participants to make a list of all the people they have harmed and be willing to make amends to them. Step 9 actually requires them to make these amends, except when doing so would injure them or others. By making this list, addicts are forced to consider the consequences of their behaviors and deal with the pain they have caused. In this way, they gain wisdom about their addictions.

God wants to bless us, and He always has a long-term perspective. He wants to bless us over the long haul. He wants life to be good for more than just a weekend. He wants to give us freedom and life. We will never know the abundant Christian life that He promises for us while we are under the power of addiction.

Get Wise!

Francis Thompson, an English poet who struggled with an addiction to opium for most of his life, wrote of how he fled from God "down the nights and down the days," but God never gave up on him. Like a great "Hound of Heaven," the Lord "with unhurrying chase, and unperturbed pace" kept pursuing him. At the end of the chase, Thompson could picture God saying to him, "Ah, fondest, blindest, weakest, I am He whom thou seekest!"[47] God never gave up on him, and He will never give up on you.

I close with this simple message: If you have become addicted to something, there is hope for you. Even if you have failed many times, there is still hope. Solomon writes, "Even if you have failed again, there is hope. For a righteous man may fall seven times and rise again, but the wicked shall fall by calamity" (Proverbs 24:16).

---

[47] Francis Thompson, "The Hound of Heaven," *The Oxford Book of English Mystical Verse* (Oxford, England, 1917).

Good people fall—sometimes seven times or 700 times. The wise always get back up.

Paul wrote, "If anyone is in Christ, he is a new creation; old things have passed away; behold, all things have become new" (2 Corinthians 5:17). As a believer in Christ, you have been set free. So embrace that new life and make the first step to conquer your addictions. Join a support group or talk to a pastor or trusted friend.

You might not conquer your addiction in a day. In my (Steve's) case, I was addicted to food for most of my life. However, through the grace of God, today I am mostly free of that addiction, and you can be free of your addiction as well. There is a saying in the get-fit-world: "Nothing tastes as good as being fit feels." The same is true of every other addiction. No high you can get from taking drugs can feel as good as being clean. No rush you can get from viewing pornography feels as good as being pure. Nothing you can buy while shopping feels as good as being out of debt.

Say no to temptations. Concentrate on the heart. Seek friends who will support you and say goodbye to friends who are a negative influence. Understand the consequences of your actions and behaviors. Be willing to seek help, and never give up hope. Wise up and live!

Wise Up About Money

There is an old fable by Aesop called "The Dog and Its Reflection" that illustrates the problem with not being wise with our possessions. In the story, a dog had come across a bone and was carrying it home to enjoy it in peace. On the way, he had to cross over a plank that had been placed over a rushing stream.

As the dog crossed the brook, he looked down and observed a wondrous sight. There, just below him in the waters, was another dog much like himself that was also holding a bone in its mouth! The dog determined that he must have that second bone and made a quick snap with his jaws at his reflection in the water. Sadly, when he opened his mouth, the bone he was carrying fell out, dropped into the stream, and was lost.

It's amazing how this simple story captures the spirit of greed we find so prevalent in our country today. We live in one of the richest nations in the world, yet most of us feel as if we don't have enough money. Interestingly, we all want the same amount: 20 percent more. Those who make $20,000 a year don't dream of making $100,000 a year—they believe it would only take about 20 percent more, or $24,000 a year, for them to be happy. Those who make $50,000 think they would be happy if they made 60,000 a year, and those who make $1 million think they would be happy if they made $1.2 million a year.

Richard Easterlin, professor of economics at University of Southern California, says that our desires adjust to our income. "At all levels of income; the typical response is that one needs 20 percent more to be happy."[48] Perhaps this explains why Americans spend $1.22 for every $1 they earn.[49] We are like the dog in the fable, always wanting just a little bit more, and often making foolish decisions to get it. Solomon states, "Better is a little with the fear of the LORD, than great treasure with trouble" (Proverbs 15:16).

The average American is richer than 93 percent of the population in the rest of the world.[50] Almost half the population of earth—more than three billion people—live on less than $2.50 a day.[51] Somehow, there has to be a way for us to be happy with the money we already have, and we find how to do so in the book of Proverbs. In fact, there are at least 101 references to money, riches, wealth, or poverty in Proverbs.[52] Money is one of the most frequently mentioned topics in the Bible.

In this chapter, we will look at some things that Proverbs has to teach us about the wise use of money.

---

[48] Richard Easterlin, cited at Penelope Trunk, "How Much Money Do You Need to Be Happy?" August 3, 2006. http://blog.penelopetrunk.com/2006/08/03/how-much-money-do-you-need-to-be-happy-hint-your-sex-life-matters-more/
[49] Jim and Jennifer Cowart, *Start This, Stop That: Do the Things That Grow Your Church* (Nashville, TN: Abingdon Press, 2012).
[50] Dylan Matthews, "The Typical American Household Is Richer Than 93 Percent of the World," The Washington Post, September 30, 2013. http://www.washingtonpost.com/blogs/wonkblog/wp/2013/09/30/the-typical-american-household-is-richer-than-93-percent-of-the-world/
[51] Anup Shah, "Poverty Facts and Stats," Global Issues, January 7, 2013. http://www.globalissues.org/article/26/poverty-facts-and-stats
[52] For one listing with verses, see "101 Biblical Proverbs About Money," Faith and Finance, November 22, 2010. http://www.faithandfinance.org/2010/11/101-biblical-proverbs-about-money/

Keep Good Records

Solomon states, "Be diligent to know the state of your flocks, and attend to your herds" (Proverbs 27:23). Notice he says to "be diligent" about this, or as the *New International Version* has it, "be sure you know." Don't just *think* you know, but be *sure* you know. Solomon writes about the "state of your flocks," which today we might refer to as "the state of your stocks." Be diligent and keep good records. You will either manage your money or your money will end up managing you.

Today, programs such as Quicken and online sites like mint.com provide tools that make money management easier than it has ever been before. These tools can help you to know the *condition* of your money—after all, you can't manage what you can't measure. However, regardless of whether you use these modern conveniences or some other system, there are four things you always should know: (1) what you owe, (2) what you own, (3) what you earn, and (4) where it all goes.[53]

Plan Your Spending

Solomon tells us that "the plans of the diligent lead surely to plenty, but those of everyone who is hasty, surely to poverty" (Proverbs 21:5). Jesus captured this same idea in the Parable of the Tower: "For which of you, intending to build a tower, does not sit down first and count the cost, whether he has enough to finish it—lest, after he has laid the foundation, and is not able to finish, all who see it begin to mock him, saying, 'This man began to build and was not able to finish'" (Luke 14:28-30).

---

[53] For more help on keeping good records, see daveramsey.com and crown.org.

Planning takes time, but it also saves time. Auguste Nélaton, the great French surgeon, once said that if he had four minutes to perform an operation to save a person's life, he would still take one minute to consider how best to do it.[54] Studies prove what common sense tells us: the more time we spend in advance planning a project, the less total time will be required to complete it.[55] Never let the day's busywork crowd out time for planning in your schedule.

One of the most important areas in which to plan concerns your spending. Plan to pay your bills, and plan to pay them on time. Solomon wrote, "Do not withhold good from those to whom it is due, when it is in the power of your hand to do so. Do not say to your neighbor, 'Go, and come back, and tomorrow I will give it,' when you have it with you" (Proverbs 3:27-28). A good rule to follow is the Golden Rule: "Whatever you want men to do to you, do also to them" (Matthew 7:12). Treat your creditors the way you would like to be treated, and pay them on time.

Note that you don't need a complicated budgeting system to make this happen. My family (Josh's) has used a simple envelope system in the past where we put money in an envelope for discretionary items such as eating out and entertainment. When the money is gone, we don't eat out anymore. It is a simple as that.

Be Cautious About Debt

The Bible does not prohibit the use of credit, but it does call for wisdom. The reason, as Solomon points out, is because this leads to

---

[54] Paul L. Tan, *Encyclopedia of 7700 Illustrations: Signs of the Times* (Garland, TX: Bible Communications, Inc., 1996).
[55] Jim George, *A Leader After God's Own Heart: 15 Ways To Lead With Strength* (Eugene, OR: Harvest House, 2012).

the rich ruling over the poor and the borrower being a "servant to the lender" (Proverbs 22:7). It comes down once again to a matter of control. Just like with addictions, we can allow our money and our spending to control us, or we can choose to have the control.

It is a sad fact of life that it is far easier to get *into* debt than it is to get *out* of it. Every week we receive pre-approved credit cards in the mail offering easy payment plans, but the reality is that there is no such thing. Payments are never easy. Sadly, many people fail to grasp this fact and their ignorance plus this easy credit has led to their financial ruin. Debt can make us slaves, rob us of our peace of mind, and hamper our ability to be generous. This is why it is so important to think long and hard before we charge up that expense card or sign that loan.

If you are in debt and you want to get out, here is some sage advice: *quit spending*. If you are in a hole and want to get out of it, you have to quit digging the hole. Wilkins Micawber, a fictional character in Charles Dickens's novel *David Copperfield,* sums it up well: "Annual income twenty pounds, annual expenditure nineteen pounds and six, result happiness. Annual income twenty pounds, annual expenditure twenty pounds and six, result misery." The point is simple: If you want to be wise, don't spend more than you make.

Some of us may be better at keeping detailed records than others, but all of us should know if we have more money or less than we did a month ago. We all should be able to say for certain if we are going deeper into debt or getting out of it. Don't be a slave to money. Wise up and stay out of debt.

Avoid Co-signing a Loan

Closely associated with the principle of being cautious about debt is avoiding co-signing a loan. Solomon states, "A man devoid of understanding shakes hands in a pledge, and becomes surety for his friend" (Proverbs 17:18). Another proverb states, "Do not be one of those who shakes hands in a pledge, one of those who is surety for debts; if you have nothing with which to pay, why should he take away your bed from under you?" (Proverbs 22:26-27).

This will be difficult for you to do if you are a compassionate person. You see a friend in need, and you know that you can help that person meet the need. It's tempting because it doesn't cost you anything on the surface—all you have to do is put your signature on the line. But God's wisdom says not to do it. There is a good reason why.

As previously stated, credit is easy to come by in this era. So it only makes sense that if a person can't get a loan, there is likely a good reason why. The person may have bad credit because of a long history of not paying his or her bills, and because past behavior is a good predictor of future action, there's a good chance that person won't pay his or her bills in the future. Guess what happens when you co-sign a loan with such a person and he or she does the same thing? That's right—if that person can't pay, you will. So just say *no* and don't do it.

This may cause tension in the relationship. The person might think that you are just being mean. The person might even accuse you of being "unchristian." After all, didn't Jesus say, "He who has two tunics, let him give to him who has none; and he who has food, let him do likewise" (Luke 3:11)? Yes, but there is a difference between helping out a person who is truly in need and enabling a person who is suffering from the consequences of his or her own bad choices. The truth is that co-signing that loan is unchristian. Wisdom says don't do it.

Enjoy What You Have

Enjoying what you have is a key principle to being wise with your money, because it will help you avoid many of the other problems we have discussed in this chapter, such as overspending and going into debt. Paul writes, "Godliness with contentment is great gain. For we brought nothing into this world, and it is certain we can carry nothing out. And having food and clothing, with these we shall be content" (1 Timothy 6: 6-8).

In Hebrews 13:5, the author sums up the main principle of contentment: "Let your conduct be without covetousness; be content with such things as you have. For He Himself has said, 'I will never leave you nor forsake you.'" Think about this for a moment. Who is richer: the one who has much and wants more, or the one who has little but believes it to be enough? Who is wealthier: the person who looks to build status in his or her own eyes, or the one who looks to the Lord and says with confidence, "My God shall supply all of my need according to His riches in glory by Christ Jesus" (Philippians 4:19)?

Sonja Lyubomirsky, a professor at the University of California, confirms what the Bible has long said: "There is now overwhelming evidence that money doesn't make people happy."[56] Money will only make you happier if you are truly destitute, but for most of us that

---

[56] Sonja Lyubomirsky, *The How of Happiness: A New Approach to Getting the Life You Want* (New York: Penguin, 2008).

isn't the case. If you have food and clothing, you would do well to follow Paul's advise and choose to be content.

Andy Stanley once asked each couple in his small group to evaluate at what point in their lives they felt the most content. Each of the couples, who were all in their mid to late forties, reported that they had been most content in the early years of their marriage when, financially, they had the least. Based on this evidence, Stanley made the following conclusion:

> Satisfying an appetite does not diminish it. It expands it. To diminish an appetite, you have to starve it. So, in the early days of marriage, when none of us in our group had a lot of extra money to do extra things, we didn't do extra things. And we were content. We were forced to starve that appetite. But once our incomes and our purchasing power began to increase, we started feeding that ugly beast. In doing so, we gave up a slice of contentment.[57]

Notice that the problem is not *seeking* to earn money but not being *satisfied* with what you have. In 1 Timothy 6:10, Paul writes, "The love of money is a root of all kinds of evil." Many have taken this to mean that it is wrong to want to get money, but that is not what Paul is saying. The issue Paul is addressing is about *wanting* it too much. When money becomes your god, sin has entered into the equation. Companies today are spending billions to make you believe you are discontent. They are trying to convince you that you cannot be happy unless you make money your god. It's a lie.

If you are having trouble in this area, here are some practical steps you can take to develop greater contentment in life. First, every day for the next week, make a list of three to five things for which you

---

[57] Andy Stanley, *How to Be Rich: It's Not What You Have, It's What You Do with What You Have* (Grand Rapids, MI: Zondervan, 2013).

are thankful. You can write these down in a notebook or find an app so you can keep the list with you at all times. Next, think about things for which you are grateful before you go to bed at night. Also write a note to someone for whom you are grateful, go to that person's house, and read it to him or her.

Author Ann Voskamp writes, "A life contemplating the blessings of Christ becomes a life acting the love of Christ."[58] Contentment grows like a muscle with use, and a continual habit of thankfulness will change your entire perspective on life. So work on forming a habit of practicing gratitude each and every day.

Save for the Future

Once you have a handle on being content with where you are and avoiding the pitfalls of debt and overspending, you can start to plan for the future. In the words of Solomon, saving for the future is exercising wisdom, "for the wise store up choice food and olive oil, but fools gulp theirs down" (Proverbs 21:20, NIV).

Of course, there is a distinction between wisely planning for the future and being a foolish hoarder. In Luke 12:16-20, Jesus tells a parable about a rich man who had an abundant harvest. "He thought within himself, saying, 'What shall I do, since I have no room to store my crops?' So he said, 'I will do this: I will pull down my barns and build greater, and there I will store all my crops and my goods. And I will say to my soul, "Soul, you have many goods laid up for many years; take your ease; eat, drink, and be merry."' But God said to him, 'Fool! This night your soul will be required of you; then whose will those things be which you have provided?'"

---

[58] Ann Voskamp, *One Thousand Gifts: A Dare to Live Fully Right Where You Are* (Grand Rapids, MI: Zondervan, 2010).

Save for the future, but don't place your security in your savings. As Jesus also said, "No one can serve two masters; for either he will hate the one and love the other, or else he will be loyal to the one and despise the other. You cannot serve God and money" (Matthew 6:24). Any time money takes first place in your life—whether that manifests itself in overspending, debt, or hoarding wealth—it has become your god.

If you want to practice wise investing for the future in the way the Bible describes, consider instructing your bank to automatically set aside a certain amount of money into a savings account. Another good idea is to follow finance expert Dave Ramsey's advice and set up a $1,000 emergency fund. Everyone has unexpected expenses. Cars break down. Refrigerators die. Emergencies happen. *Life* happens. So be ready.

Give Obediently Back to God

A final step in being wise with our money is to give obediently back to God. The Bible often refers to this as the "tithe" or "firstfruits" of our labor, as we find in Proverbs 3:9-10: "Honor the LORD with your possessions, and with the firstfruits of all your increase; so your barns will be filled with plenty, and your vats will overflow with new wine."

The word "tithe" means one-tenth of something, and it was something that God commanded His people to give in Leviticus 27:30: "All the tithe of the land, whether of the seed of the land or of the fruit of the tree, is the LORD's. It is holy to the LORD." Today, Christians still follow this practice by giving 10 percent of their income to their local church, and they also give offerings in addition to their tithes.

The word "first fruits" refers to the fact that the Israelites gave this portion to the Lord *first* before anything else. Robert Morris, pastor of Gateway Church, shows the importance of this concept for us today when he writes, "The most important part of the tithe is not that it's 10 percent of our income, but that it's the first 10 percent. God didn't tell Israel to conquer all of the Promised Land and then give Him one city. He told the people to give Him all of the silver and the gold from Jericho. Why? Because it was the first one, and the rest would be blessed if they gave the first one!"[59] Giving God the first fruits of our labor shows that we put Him first in our lives.

In my (Josh's) own life, I have found that if I wait until the end of the month to give to God, there is never anything left to give. That kind of giving does not honor God, so I make it automatic. I have instructed my bank to regularly send a check for my giving. No muss, no fuss. I don't think about it or stress about it. I don't decide every month whether or not I'm going to do it. It just happens. You can do the same. Put the payment on autopilot. Do whatever it takes to give to God first.

It's interesting to note that the number one topic Solomon deals with in the book of Proverbs is not about how to *get* money but how to *give* money. Why is this? Why is giving so important to God? It is not because He needs money. In Psalm 50:10, God says, "For every beast of the forest is Mine, and the cattle on a thousand hills." In other words, God is rich and doesn't need anything from us. The reason He wants us to give is for *our* own good, not His own. God knows that giving changes our hearts, because when we give, it loosens the stranglehold that materialism has over us.

---

[59] Robert Morris, "What Every Pastor Needs to Know About Giving," Ministry Today. http://ministrytodaymag.com/index.php/ministry-leadership/finance/15793-what-every-pastor-needs-to-know-about-giving

If you want to love God more than you do right now, then give more than you do right now. Your heart will always follow your pocketbook. If you are primarily investing in material possessions, that will become your focus in life. If you are investing in God's work, that will become your focus and your heart will follow. Give more and you will find yourself loving God (and others) more.

Get Wise!

In the end, we see that God wants us to be *rich,* but He defines that term differently than we do. To God, being rich means being content with the blessings that He has given. God's means of making us rich is by making us wise in the area of money and generous with our giving. Solomon states, "The generous soul will be made rich, and he who waters will also be watered himself" (Proverbs 11:25).

Giving is good for you. This is what the Bible teaches, and it is what modern science confirms. Here are seven reasons why this is true:

1. **It keeps stress in check.** Research shows that being stingy is linked with higher levels of the stress hormone cortisol. In studies, the more money people chose to keep, the greater shame they felt—and the higher were their cortisol levels. While some stress is good, chronically high levels of stress have been linked to a number of health ills.

2. **Your happiness at work depends on it.** One study by the University of Wisconsin-Madison shows that being altruistic improves wellbeing at work, makes people feel more committed to their work, and makes them less likely to quit. According to researcher Donald Moynihan,

"Helping others makes us happier. Altruism is not a form of martyrdom, but operates for many as part of a healthy psychological reward system."

3. **It's beneficial to the greater good.** Researchers at the University of Pennsylvania found that when people are generous, it leads to greater cooperation, greater benefits for everyone involved, and greater success overall. Researcher Alexander Stewart noted, "You might think being generous would be a stupid thing to do . . . but if people all play generously, they all benefit from each other's generosity."

4. **You will enjoy more years of life.** Researchers from the University of Buffalo found a link between giving and a lower risk of early death. The findings show that helping others—whether that is by helping run errands, watching people's children, or giving them a lift somewhere is linked with a decreased mortality risk.

5. **It keeps the cycle of "good" going.** According to a 2012 study by *Psychological Science,* when people think about the times they've given of themselves, it makes them feel selfless and encourages them to help others. In other words, when a person reflects on the times he or she has helped others, it makes that person want to help them again—and what can be better than that?

6. **It will strengthen your marriage.** A study from the National Marriage Project reports that generosity is a key factor for a happy marriage. Elizabeth Marquardt, associate editor of the report, states that people "are happier in their

marriages when they make a regular effort to serve their spouse in small ways—from making them a cup of coffee, to giving them a back rub after a long day, to going out of their way to be affectionate or forgiving."

7. **It will promote your mental health.** In a review published by the *BMC Public Health* journal, researchers found that volunteering not only improves a person's wellbeing and life satisfaction but is also linked with decreased depression and a lower risk of early death. The researchers stated, "This review suggests that bio-social and cultural factors may influence both a willingness to engage in volunteering, as well as the benefits that might accrue."[60]

People who want to be wise with their money do not allow it to control them. They believe that when they bring their tithes to God, He will open "the windows of heaven and pour out . . . such blessing that there will not be room enough to receive it" (Malachi 3:10). They give generously as a way to "seek first the kingdom of God and His righteousness," believing that "all these things shall be added" to them (Matthew 6:33). They understand that God promises to meet their needs if they put Him first.

Keep track of your money and what you spend. Be cautious about incurring debt and enabling others to incur debt. Enjoy what you have and save for the future. Above all, put God first by giving obediently back to Him, and be generous with the resources that He has given to you. Be wise with your money and live well.

---

[60] Amanda L. Chan, "Seven Science-Backed Reasons Why Generosity Is Good for Your Health," The Huffington Post, January 23, 2014. http://www.huffingtonpost.com/2013/12/01/generosity-health_n_4323727.html

Wise Up About Work

Michael Jordan was one of the greatest basketball players to ever play the game—if not *the* greatest player of all time. However, he didn't gain his success on the court through genetics alone (though that certainly played a factor) or by just showing up to the games. No, Michael Jordan perfected his skills through hard work.

According to Phil Jackson, Jordan's long-time coach with the Chicago Bulls, the star player never took anything about his game for granted. When he first came to the NBA in 1984, Jordan's primary style was to drive to the basket, and his outside shooting wasn't up to pro standards. So, during the offseason, he shot hundreds of buckets every day. Eventually, he became an excellent three-point threat.

Jordan also struggled with defense, so he spent hours studying his opponents, learning their moves, and planning how to stop them. He worked hard to perfect his footwork and his balance. The result of all this effort? During his 15 seasons in the NBA, Jordan won 6 NBA championships, was the NBA's most valuable player five times, was an NBA All-Star 14 times, led the league in scoring for 10 years, was the Associated Press athlete of the year three times, was the Chicago Bulls' all-time leading scorer, and earned dozens of other awards.[61]

---

[61] Phil Jackson, "Michael and Me," *Inside Stuff,* June/July 1998. http://www.nba.com/jordan/is_philonmj.html

Michael Jordan became great because he had an amazing work ethic. In many ways, he was like the ant Solomon describes in Proverbs 6:6-8: "Consider the ant's ways and be wise, which, having no captain, overseer or ruler, provides her supplies in the summer, and gathers her food in the harvest." Jordan worked hard both on the court in front of the crowds and off the court when no one was watching. His hard work paid off and made him successful at his chosen profession.

How many of us do the same? How many of us stay late or put in the extra hour when needed to get the job done? On the flip side, how many of us put in *too many hours* at work at the expense of our family and friends? Proverbs tells us that there is a way to work wise, and we do that not only by working hard but also by working well, working smart, and working according to our gifting. Let's take a look at just a few of the verses in Proverbs about our work.

Recognize the Value of Work

Solomon writes, "In all labor there is profit, but idle chatter leads only to poverty" (Proverbs 14:23). We were created in the image of God (see Genesis 1:27), and He is always at work in the world (see John 5:17). When God placed Adam and Eve in the Garden of Eden, He commanded them to "fill the earth and subdue it; have dominion over the fish of the sea, over the birds of the air, and over every living thing that moves on the earth" (Genesis 1:28). One of the first tasks He gave to Adam was to name each living creature (see 2:19). So, from the very beginning, God intended humans to work. As a hammer was made to drive nails, we were made to work.

Paul writes, "Whatever you do, do it heartily, as to the Lord and not to men" (Colossians 3:23). Notice he says *whatever* you do. All work is

God's work. He wants preachers to preach, singers to sing, teachers to teach, and coaches to coach. He wants you to do your work—whether that is laying bricks, preparing sermons, helping the needy, or anything else—with all your heart. As Martin Luther said, "The works of monks and priests . . . do not differ one whit in the sight of God from the works of the rustic laborer in the field or the woman going about her household tasks, but that all works are measured before God by faith alone."[62]

There is actually a link between the sacred and the secular when it comes to work. Author Dan Miller states, "There is a Hebrew word, *avodah*, from which come both the words 'work' and 'worship.' To the Hebrew man, his Thursday morning activities were just as much an expression of worship as being in the synagogue on the Sabbath. Nothing in Scripture depicts the Christian life as divided into sacred and secular parts. Rather, it shows a unified life, one of wholeness, in which everything we do is service to God, including our daily work, whatever that may be."[63]

Unfortunately, many Christians today do not see this connection. Like the culture around them, they see their work as something they must endure so they can get to the weekend. Perhaps you have seen those bumper stickers that say, "I'd rather be camping" or, "I'd rather be fishing." Ever see one that says, "I'd rather be working"? There is even a restaurant named TGIF: Thank God It's Friday. We thank God it's Friday because we have a weekend off from work. Not many people thank God for Monday when we get to go back to work.

---

[62] Martin Luther, quoted in Dan Miller, *48 Days to the Work You Love* (Nashville, TN: B&H, 2010).
[63] Miller, *48 Days to the Work You Love.*

God has put each and every one of us on earth for a purpose, and He wants us to work to achieve the goals He has established for us. He knows that work is good for us—and modern science actually confirms that fact. Hungarian psychologist Mihaly Csikszentmihalyi states that each of us is happiest in life when we experience what he calls "flow" moments, which are those times when we are so completely absorbed with the activity at hand that we focus on nothing else. For instance, as he writes:

> Imagine that you are skiing down a slope and your full attention is focused on the movements of your body, the position of the skis, the air whistling past your face, and the snow-shrouded trees running by. There is no room in your awareness for conflicts or contradictions; you know that a distracting thought or emotion might get you buried face down in the snow. The run is so perfect that you want it to last forever. . . . Moments such as these provide flashes of intense living against the dull background of everyday life.[64]

What research shows is that people experience these flow moments more often when they are on the job than when they are off it. Psychologist Martin Seligman explains, "Work can be prime time for flow because, unlike leisure, it builds many of the conditions of flow into itself. There are usually clear goals and rules of performance. There is frequent feedback about how well or poorly we are doing. Work usually encourages concentration and minimizes distractions, and in many cases it matches the difficulties to your talents and even your strengths. As a result, people often feel more engaged at work than they do at home."[65]

---

[64] "Finding Flow: A Review of the Book 'Finding Flow' by Mihaly Csikszentmihalyi," Psychology Today, June 14, 2012. http://www.psychologytoday.com/articles/199707/finding-flow

[65] Martin E. P. Seligman, *Authentic Happiness: Using the New Positive Psychology to Realize Your Potential for Lasting Fulfillment* (New York: Atria Books, 2004).

Science and the Bible agree: work is good for us. As Proverbs tells us, "The hand of the diligent makes rich," and, "the hand of the diligent will rule" (10:4; 12:24).

Work Hard

Solomon has this to say to the lazy person: "How long will you slumber, O sluggard? When will you rise from your sleep? A little sleep, a little slumber, a little folding of the hands to sleep—so shall your poverty come on you like a prowler, and your need like an armed man" (Proverbs 6:9-11). Notice the phrase, "a little sleep, a little slumber." For the slacker, that is how it starts—a little compromise here or there. Satan will rarely tempt us in the big areas; rather, he will get us to compromise our ethics gradually. The road to poverty is paved with a little bit of slacking off.

We were all not only made to work but also to work *hard*. Paul said of himself and his colleagues, "We labor, working with our own hands" (1 Corinthians 4:12). The Greek word translated as "working" in this verse suggests the kind of effort that makes one tired. It is the kind of work that makes a person sweat. In other places, it is translated as "weary" and "toil." Paul actually warned believers to stay away from those who were idle: "We command you, brothers and sisters, to keep away from every believer who is idle . . . for we were not idle when we were with you, nor did we eat anyone's food without paying for it. On the contrary, we worked night and day, laboring and toiling so that we would not be a burden to any of you" (2 Thessalonians 3:6-8, NIV).

Both of us travel a good deal in our work. While some people see travel as a glamorous thing, much of the time it is just plain hard work. Travel requires us to put in long days getting from here to there, sitting in airports, waiting on delays, and driving to distant places. When we arrive, it is seldom an exotic location with lots of sightseeing. Usually, the trip involves checking into a hotel, visiting a church's fellowship hall, checking out, and returning back home again. Sometimes people ask, "Doesn't traveling make you tired?" Of course it does. That is why we call it work!

Solomon states, "He who tills his land will be satisfied with bread, but he who follows frivolity is devoid of understanding" (Proverbs 12:11). If you want to be wise and satisfied with your life, choose to work hard.

Work Well

Hard work is important, but hard work alone is not enough. To be truly wise, we must also work with *excellence* and strive to become good at what we do. Like Michael Jordan, we need to work hard to improve the areas in which we lack so we can be the best in our chosen professions. Proverbs 22:29 states, "Do you see a man who excels in his work? He will stand before kings; he will not stand before unknown men." The word "excels" suggests working with excellence and having extraordinary expertise in some area.[66] It means we cross every *T* and dot every *I*.

I (Josh) am regularly in churches where the people are praying for the blessing of God. They are praying for revival and a mighty movement of the Holy Spirit to come over the congregation. I find that all well and good, and of course I applaud their efforts. However, I often wonder what they are doing to make that happen. I look around and think, *Wouldn't it be great if someone came in to*

---

[66] Warren Baker and Gene Carpenter, *The Complete Word Study Dictionary: Old Testament* (Chattanooga, TN: AMG Publishers, 2003).

tune the piano? Wouldn't it be great if someone did something about the landscaping? Wouldn't it be great if there weren't typos in the PowerPoint slides? Wouldn't it be great if I could figure out what the preacher was trying to say? It would be great if the people who did God's work did it with skill.

Without exception, I find that the churches where the lost are being saved, the spirit is vibrant, and the kingdom of God is expanding are those churches where the work of God is being done with excellence. Blessings generally do not come about because of arbitrary factors or just blind luck. The blessing of God normally comes because of hard work done well.

Bill Hybels writes, "We must fight for excellence because it is excellence that honors God. It is excellence that inspires people. And it is excellence that means trouble for the enemy of our souls."[67] To be wise, we must work hard *and* work well.

Work Smart

In Luke 16, Jesus told a parable about a manager who called his steward to account for his actions. Even though the steward was unjust, the manager commended him because he was shrewd. In other words, the servant was prudent, sensible, and practically wise in his relationships.[68] Part of working hard and working well involves being shrewd in our efforts. It requires taking advantage of the resources that are available to us and using them to maximize our efforts.

---

[67] Bill Hybels, *Axiom: Powerful Leadership Proverbs* (Grand Rapids, MI: Zondervan, 2008).
[68] Spiros Zodhiates, *The Complete Word Study Dictionary: New Testament* (Chattanooga, TN: AMG Publishers, 2003).

The story of a missionary who worked deep in the Amazon jungle illustrates this idea. For years, he would travel three days by boat to reach his destination, and it would take him another three days to row out. One day, an organization approached him and said that they could get him there via air in only three hours. But the missionary turned them down. "This is what I was called to do," he said.

In fact, this was not what the missionary was called to do at all. He had been called to preach the gospel, and by not taking the organization up on their offer, he was wasting six days of rowing that he could have used to fulfill his mission. Any time that technology can help us do a better job, we would do well to take advantage of it.

Working smart also involves knowing when to *stop* working. While we all want to do our best, there comes a time when we need to quit working, go home, and do the work of relating to our families. God Himself set this model for us when He rested on the seventh day after creation (see Genesis 2:2), and He commanded that His people also observe a day of rest. "Six days you shall labor and do all your work, but the seventh day is the Sabbath of the LORD your God. In it you shall do no work" (Exodus 20:9-10). Six days on, and one day off. That is God's plan.

The media is filled with stories of businesspeople who have missed this important point and put in ridiculously long hours at work. Howard Shultz, CEO of Starbucks, gets to work by 6 AM, stays until 7 PM, and works late into the night from home. Mark Cuban, owner of the Dallas Mavericks, didn't take a vacation for seven years while starting his first business. Jeffrey Immelt, CEO of GE, put in 100-hour workweeks for 24 years. Marissa Mayer, former executive at Google, regularly pulled all-nighters while working for the company. In an interview, she said she managed her schedule by sleeping under her desk and being "strategic" about her showers.[69]

This is not what God had in mind for us in our work. Wise people don't work themselves to death or ignore their families. So work hard, work well, but above all, work smart.

Work According to Your Gifting

God has given each of us different gifts, talents, personalities, and interests, and if we want to be wise, we need to work according to those giftings. This applies not only to our spiritual gifts but also our natural abilities. In 1 Corinthians 12:14-18, Paul explains how all of our gifts work together. Eugene Peterson summarizes it:

> A body isn't just a single part blown up into something huge. It's all the different-but-similar parts arranged and functioning together. If Foot said, "I'm not elegant like Hand, embellished with rings; I guess I don't belong to this body," would that make it so? If Ear said, "I'm not beautiful like Eye, limpid and expressive; I don't deserve a place on the head," would you want to remove it from the body? If the body was all eye, how could it hear? If all ear, how could it smell? As it is, we see that God has carefully placed each part of the body right where he wanted it (MSG).

The Gallup Organization did a poll where they asked people whether they agree with the statement, "At work, I have the opportunity to do what I do best every day." Of those surveyed, not one person who "strongly disagreed" or "disagreed" with this

---

[69] Max Nisen, "16 People Who Worked Incredibly Hard to Succeed," Business Insider, September 5, 2012. http://www.businessinsider.com/16-people-who-worked-incredibly-hard-to-succeed-2012-9?op=1

statement was emotionally engaged on the job. In stark contrast, studies indicate that those who focused on their strengths every day were six times more likely to be engaged in their jobs and three times more likely to report having an excellent quality of life in general.[70] They were also 50 percent more likely to work in teams that had lower employee turnover, 38 percent more likely to work in highly productive teams, and 44 percent more likely to work in teams with higher customer satisfaction scores.

For me (Josh), life gradually moved me toward the sweet spot of my gifting. I started out as a minister of education, but my job satisfaction was about a 5 out of 10. I always had a heart for ministry outside of the local church, so I published a book, and the phone started ringing. I started doing conferences based on the books I published. This was definitely a step closer to my gifting, but I missed connecting with people. Now I get to do a bit of both. I spent a good deal of my time writing, which I love. I spend some time traveling, which I enjoy. I pastor a small church, which gives me an outlet to use my spiritual gifts of teaching and leadership. Life just keeps getting better and better for me as I work in the sweet spot of my gifting.

As employees, it is our responsibility to do what we can to move toward the sweet spot of what is satisfying work for us. As leaders, it is our responsibility to make our working environment a little "slice of heaven." Dennis Bakke, co-founder and CEO of AES, a large energy company that grew to more than $8 billion in annual revenue and more than 40,000 employees, states:

> God intended that the workplace be beautiful, exciting, and satisfying. Work was to be filled with joy. Work was a major

---

[70] Tom Rath, *StrengthsFinder 2.0* (New York: Gallup Press, 2007).

reason for our creation. It was intended to be an important act of worship. It was one of the most significant ways in which we could honor our Creator. From this perspective it is our responsibility to do whatever we can to make the modern workplace the way it was intended to be. While I realize the world is not the Garden of Eden, I do believe it is incumbent on those of us in leadership roles to do whatever we can to make the workplace as fun and successful as we can.[71]

Of course, it will never *be* heaven—it will always be work—but the closer we can get toward the place God wants us to be, the more effective we will be. As we move closer and closer into our giftings in our work, we will both enjoy what we do more and be better at it. After all, it is hard to be really good at something you don't truly enjoy.

Get Wise!

A tourist once visited the national capital and entered one of the many department buildings. He went into a large room off the lobby, where he expected to see many clerks working behind the desks that were there. However, to his surprise he could find no one. As he wandered through the room, he came across a janitor who was dusting and cleaning. He approached the janitor and asked, "Say, could you tell me how many people work here?" The janitor looked up and said, "About half of them."

It is true that there are two kinds of people in this world: those who work hard, and those who are glad to let them. The Bible teaches that it is wise to work and to work hard, well, smart, and according

---

[71] Dennis W. Bakke, *Joy at Work: A Revolutionary Approach to Fun on the Job* (Seattle, WA: PVG, 2005).

to our giftings. Work is not a punishment. God created it before the Fall, and everything He created He said was good (see Genesis 1).

Colin Powell once said, "There are no secrets to success. It is the result of preparation, hard work, and learning from failure."[72] Proverbs tells us that those who embrace this view of work can expect wealth (see 10:4), positions of authority (see 12:24), satisfaction in their soul (see 13:4), and honor (see 22:29). So don't be a fool when it comes to your work. Wise up and follow God's path to success.

---

[72] Colin Powell, quoted in Oren Harari, *The Leadership Secrets of Colin Powell* (New York: McGraw-Hill, 2002), p. 164.

Wise Up About Parenting

Carlos Irwin Estévez, better known by his stage name Charlie Sheen, rose to fame in the 1980s after appearing in successful films such as *Platoon, Ferris Bueller's Day Off, Wall Street, Young Guns, Eight Men Out,* and *Major League.* In the 2000s, he became known for his television roles on *Spin City* and *Two and a Half Men.* However, everything began to publicly unravel for him in 2011. It began in January when Sheen, who was undergoing his third substance rehabilitation program in twelve months, made derogatory comments about Chuck Lorre, the creator of *Two and a Half Men.* Warner Bros. banned Sheen from entering its production lot and dismissed him in March.[73] Sheen went on to remain critical of Lorre, and even went so far as to file a wrongful termination suit.[74] He also started making bizarre statements to the press, suggesting that he was a "warlock" who had "tiger blood" and "Adonis DNA." In one interview, he said, "I'm tired of pretending I'm not special. I'm tired of pretending I'm not a . . . rock star from Mars."[75]

Martin Sheen, Charlie's father, said watching his son lead a similarly decadent life to the one that he had led during his young film

---

[73] Ed Pilkington, "*Two and a Half* Men Axed After Rant Leaves Sheen Looking a Proper Charlie," *The Guardian*, February 25, 2011, http://www.theguardian.com/culture/2011/feb/25/two-and-a-half-men-sheen-charlie; Kat Angus, "Charlie Sheen Banned from Warner Bros. Lot," *Calgary Herald*, February 28, 2011.
[74] Nallie Andreeva, "FIRED! Charlie Sheen Axed From *Two and a Half Men*, He Fires Back and Vows to Sue," *Deadline.com*, March 7, 2011.
[75] Torie Bosch, "Charlie Sheen Interviews: Tiger Blood, Adonis DNA and Charlie Sheen the Drug Videos," Aolnews.com, February 28, 2011.

career filled him with remorse. He worried that he had learned to be a father too late, and he particularly regretted failing to share his faith. "I never lost my faith," he said, "but I felt for a time that I had outgrown the church. Now it is a bone of contention in my soul that I did not share my faith with my kids, as my parents did with me. It was a source of grace when I needed it. I have been greatly nurtured and inspired by my faith."[76]

Martin Sheen is not alone in his sentiments. There are many parents today who look back at how they raised their children and wonder if they could have done things differently. Likewise, there are many parents currently raising kids who are asking themselves if they are doing everything they can to instill godly values in their offspring. They wonder if they are following the words of Proverbs 22:6: "Train up a child in the way he should go, and when he is old he will not depart from it."

Of course, when you read statements such as this in the book of Proverbs, you have to remember what we first stated in the introduction: these are not *promises* but *proverbs*—short, pithy statements about the way things usually work. As John MacArthur states, Proverbs 22:6 doesn't represent "a promise for Christian parents to claim that will guarantee their children will never depart from the way of truth."[77] You could very well be a caring and dedicated parent—one who does "everything right"—and still have children who give up the faith or get into trouble.[78] Even Franklin

---

[76] Martin Sheen, quoted in Craig Brian Larson and Phyllis Ten Elshof, *1001 Illustrations That Connect* (Grand Rapids, MI: Zondervan Publishing House, 2008), p. 292, from an interview published in the *Electronic Telegraph (Telegraph UK)*.
[77] John MacArthur, *Successful Christian Parenting: Raising Your Child with Care, Compassion, and Common Sense* (Bedford, TX: Word Publishing, 1998), p. 20.
[78] Paul E. Koptak, *Proverbs, The NIV Application Commentary* (Grand Rapids, MI: Zondervan, 2003), p. 517.

Graham, the son of evangelist Billy Graham, wandered from the Lord for quite some time.

Nothing brings us greater joy than our kids, nothing brings us greater heartache than our kids, and no arena of life calls for more wisdom than how we raise our kids. So, let's look at a few essentials about how to wisely raise our children in the way that will most likely bring us joy and not break our hearts.

Recognize That Parenting Is Difficult

A recent survey conducted by the Pew Research Center revealed that most people today think parenting is more difficult than it was 20 or 30 years ago. Seventy percent of those surveyed believed it was more difficult to be a mother, and 60 percent said it was more difficult to be a father. More than half said that parents are not doing as good of a job as they did a generation ago.[79]

There are several reasons for this. First, parents today lack the support of extended family. In the past, grandparents, aunts, and uncles were around to help, but in our mobile world this support system is often far away. In addition, 26 percent of children are being raised in single-parent homes (in the African-American community, the number is 72 percent), and many kids are being raised in blended families.[80] Forty-two percent of adults have a

[79] "Motherhood Today: Tougher Challenges, Less Success," Pew Research Social and Demographic Trends, May 2, 2007. http://www.pewsocialtrends.org/2007/05/02/motherhood-today-tougher-challenges-less-success/
[80] "72 Percent of Black Kids Raised by Single Parent, 25 Percent Overall in U.S.," NewsOne, April 27, 2011. http://newsone.com/1195075/children-single-parents-u-s-american/

"step-relationship" (are either a step-parent, a step- or half-sibling, or a stepchild). This translates to roughly 95 million adults.[81]

The Internet is another factor adding to the challenges of parenting. Today, sinful influences such as porn and illegal drugs are just a mouse click away. Parents also have to worry about online predators, as one in five teenagers who regularly log on to the Internet report having received an unwanted sexual solicitation via the web. Online harassment and bullying has grown 50 percent in just the last five years—and continues to increase.[82] Without the proper precautions in place, children can easily find porn and encounter other dangers online.

Parents today are busier than ever before, which creates many difficulties for mothers and fathers to find time to connect with their children. A number of years ago, Robert Schuller, founder of the Crystal Cathedral in California, discovered firsthand how this can affect a family. Schuller was on a whirlwind book tour, visiting eight cities in four days while juggling his duties at the church. As he was going over his schedule for his return home, his secretary reminded him that he had an appointment with the winner of a raffle. Schuller received a wakeup call when he realized that the winner was his teenage daughter. The $500 she had bid to have lunch with him represented her entire life savings.[83]

---

[81] "A Portrait of Stepfamilies," Pew Research Social and Demographic Trends, January 13, 2011. http://www.pewsocialtrends.org/2011/01/13/a-portrait-of-stepfamilies/

[82] "Internet Safety Statistics and Findings," Safe Wave, 2006. Data taken from the 2006 Report from the National Center for Missing and Exploited Children. http://www.safewave.org/index.php?option=com_content&task=view&id=353&Itemid=300

[83] Steve Farrar, *Standing Tall: How a Man Can Protect His Family* (Sisters, OR: Multnomah, 2006).

Parenting today is difficult. The sooner we recognize this fact, the sooner we will wise up when it comes to raising our kids.

Monitor Your Children's Hearts

In Proverbs 23:26, a wise parent encouraged his child to "give me your heart, and let your eyes observe my ways." Wise parents constantly monitor the hearts of their children to see whether they are open or closed. They understand that having enough of the right rules is important, but not nearly as important as maintaining a relationship with their kids. They understand that rules without relationship equal rebellion.

When our children rebel, the first thing we need to do is evaluate our relationship with them. Author Gary Smalley states that this key to our children's heart and that the most prevalent cause of disharmony within a home is a "closed spirit," or a breach in the relationship. He writes:

> When I was a child, I enjoyed observing sea anemones on the California coast. . . . About four or five inches in diameter, they look like colorful flowers with soft, wavy tentacles. But I noticed an interesting phenomenon. Sometimes I'd take a stick and poke one of them. Immediately the sea anemone would withdraw its sensitive tentacles and close up until it became a shell. It was similar to a beautiful flower closing. Now it was protected from further injury.
>
> What happens with the sea anemone illustrates what happens to a person when he is offended. . . . When a person is offended, he closes up. When his spirit closes, it in turn closes his soul and body. If the spirit is open, so are the soul and body. In other words, when the spirits of two people are open, they enjoy talking (soul) and touching (body). If the spirit closes, the soul

and body close to the same degree.[84]

You can tell if your children have a closed spirit by observing their body language, posture, and facial expressions. Closed children tend to stop communicating with others on a meaningful level and may frequently argue, withdraw, or be unresponsive to affection. They may also rebel and act out.

So, how do you reopen your children's heart? First, stop yelling and using harsh language. Convey that they are important to you and that you are willing to listen to what they have to say. Seek to understand their pain and see things from their point of view. Recognize any offense you committed in your attitude and actions and seek forgiveness for those faults. Finally, don't be afraid to show affection. Wise parents are not afraid to reach out and hug their kids, even if they know the child will pull away.[85]

Teach Your Kids About Life

In Proverbs 1:8, Solomon writes, "My son, hear the instruction of your father, and do not forsake the law of your mother." Parents are *teachers*, not law enforcement officials. They provide rules and consequences, but they are fundamentally educators to their children. This includes sharing the Bible with them, but it goes beyond just family devotions. It is a lifestyle of non-stop teaching, 24/7, 365 days a year.

Moses taught the Israelites about this in Deuteronomy 6:6-9, where he said, "These words which I command you today shall be in your

---

[84] Gary Smalley, *The Key to Your Child's Heart* (Nashville, TN: Thomas Nelson, 2003).
[85] "Attitudes: Steps to Opening Your Child's Spirit," (review of *The Key to Your Child's Heart*), iMom, 2007. http://www.imom.com/attitudes-steps-to-opening-your-childs-spirit/

heart. You shall teach them diligently to your children, and shall talk of them when you sit in your house, when you walk by the way, when you lie down, and when you rise up. You shall bind them as a sign on your hand, and they shall be as frontlets between your eyes. You shall write them on the doorposts of your house and on your gates."

You can't instill values with just a brief two-minute bedtime story. You have to live it with your kids around the clock and instruct them through a thousand and more casual conversations. Look for ways to bring up important subjects with your kids. Did you hear that some teenager got pregnant? Talk about the dangers of premarital sex with your kids. Read of a drunk driving accident? Talk to your kids about alcohol abuse. Bring the subject up later and review the lesson. Make sure your kids know how you see and interpret life.

Also talk to your kids about money and how to spend and save it. I (Josh) like to say that money is of medium importance—it is not as important as topics such as love, but it still matters. So talk to your kids and share your values as it relates to acquiring possessions, working hard, and being generous with your resources.

Correct Your Children When Necessary

Children are not blank slates. They are born into this world foolish and as sinners. After all, no parent has to teach his or her children how to be *bad*—they just do it by nature. For this reason, the Bible instructs us to use the rod of correction on our kids to drive the foolishness from them. Proverbs has much to say on the subject:

> Foolishness is bound up in the heart of a child; the rod of correction will drive it far from him (Proverbs 22:15).

Do not withhold correction from a child, for if you beat him with a rod, he will not die. You shall beat him with a rod, and deliver his soul from hell (Proverbs 23:13–14).

Correct your son, and he will give you rest; yes, he will give delight to your soul (Proverbs 29:17).

Note that Proverbs doesn't say *threats* will change behavior. You can threaten your kids all day, but if you don't follow it up with action, they will never have a reason to change their behavior. Nor does nagging change behavior—it only makes you and your kids miserable. Screaming is also ineffective. As we discussed in chapter 4, parents who yell at their kids only end up having more problems with them.

Only *consequences* shape behavior. I (Josh) have known some of the most soft-spoken parents who could merely raise one eyebrow and their children would respond. They had no need to threaten, nag, or yell, because they had trained their children that what was coming next was action. Their kids understood that when that eyebrow was raised, it meant their parent was getting ready to enforce some consequences.

In his book *Have a New Kid by Friday*, Kevin Leman sets up an interesting scenario to illustrate how consequences shape behavior. He asks readers to imagine picking up their child from school and discovering that he or she is in a foul mood. All the child wants to do is argue. At one point, the child actually yells, "I hate you!" Leman says that as a parent, you have several choices on how to respond:

- React by giving the child a tongue-lashing of your own.
- Ignore the comment and the child.

- Do something to nip this kind of behavior in the bud . . . for good.

Leman notes that parents who react in kind will end up leaving the car feeling ugly and out of sorts. They will feel bad about how they acted for the rest of the day. As far as the child is concerned, he or she will probably go to his or her room and sulk. Eventually, one or both will end up apologizing. If the parents feel guilty enough, they might give the child some treats to express their remorse.

Parents who choose to ignore their child might find that tactic working for a while—until the kid needs something from them. If that child is four years old, the strategy will work only seconds, because there are many things in the house that the child can't reach. Lehman notes that if the behavior is not addressed, parents will only end up fuming at their kid . . . and probably taking it out on the dog.

But what if parents decide to do something truly revolutionary? What if they decide enough is enough and they are going to nip their kid's behavior in the bud? For good? Lehman shares the following illustration of a mom and her disrespectful son, named Matthew, to show how this might work:

Once she [the mom] and Matthew got in the house, she didn't say a word. She went about her business, putting away the shopping bags from the car. After a few minutes, Matthew wandered into the kitchen. Usually chocolate chip cookies and milk awaited him there. It was his routine after-preschool snack.

"Mommy, where are my cookies and milk?" he asked, looking at the usual place on the kitchen counter.

"We're not having cookies and milk today," she said matter-of-factly. Then she turned her back on the child ... and walked into another room.

Did Matthew say to himself, *Well, I guess I'll have to do without that today?* No, because children are creatures of habit. So what did Matthew do? He followed his mother to the next room.

"Mommy, I don't understand. We always have cookies and milk after preschool."

Mom looked him in the eye and said, "Mommy doesn't feel like getting you cookies and milk today." She turned and walked into another room.

By now, Matthew was like an NFL Quarterback on Sunday afternoon—scrambling to get to the goal. He followed his mom into the next room. "But, Mommy, this has never happened before." There was panic in his voice. He was starting to tremble. "I don't understand."

Mom now knew that Matthew was ready to hear what she had to say. It was the teachable moment: the moment when reality enters the picture and makes an impact on the child's mind and heart. It's the time when a parent has to give her child the straight skinny.

"We are not having milk and cookies today because Mommy doesn't like the way you talked to me in the car." Again, Mom turned to walk away.

But before she took three steps, Matthew had a giant meltdown.

He ran toward his mother and grabbed her leg (after all, he is part of the ankle-biter battalion). He was crying profusely. "I'm sorry, Mommy! I'm sorry. I shouldn't have said that."

Time for another wonderful opportunity. The mom accepted Matthew's apology, gave him a hug, and reminded him that she loved him. She also told him how she felt when he talked to her like that. Three minutes later, things were patched up, and she let Matthew out of her embrace. She began again to go about her work.

What did she hear next from Matthew? "Mommy, can I have my milk and cookies now?"

It was the moment she feared. She steeled her courage and said calmly, "Honey, I told you no. We are not going to have milk and cookies today."

Matthew was stunned. He opened his mouth to argue, then walked away sadly.

Let me ask you: will that little boy think next time before he disses his mother? [86]

Let me take a stab at that last question: it depends. It depends on the kid. Some kids are more stubborn than others. For some kids, you have to deliver consequences multiple times before they get it. Yet kids are smart. They will learn to behave for the wise parent who consistently delivers consequences.

There is a difference between correction and punishment. Punishment is just to inflict pain. Correction is about shaping behavior. Wise parents don't punish their kids just to cause pain. They correct to shape behavior.

Build Your Kids' Confidence

As we are correcting our children, we have to be careful not to discourage them or make them feel like failures. Remember that *rules* without *relationship* only leads to *rebellion*. Paul writes, "Fathers, do not provoke your children, lest they become

---

[86] Kevin Leman, *Have a New Kid by Friday: How to Change Your Child's Attitude, Behavior and Character in Five Days* (Grand Rapids, MI: Revell, 2008).

discouraged" (Colossians 3:21; see also Ephesians 6:4). We are to catch our kids doing something *right* more often than we catch them doing *wrong*. When we find them doing something right, we are wise to praise them and/or reward them.

There are two kinds of consequences that shape behavior: pain and pleasure. It is the old carrot and stick analogy, and we need both. After all, it is the way our heavenly Father parents us. In Deuteronomy 30:15, Moses said to the Israelites, "See, I have set before you today life and good, death and evil." Notice the carrot and stick: if the Israelites wanted life and good (the carrot), they needed to choose obedience. If they didn't choose obedience, death and evil (the stick) would follow.

One of the biggest ways to destroy the confidence of your children is to become a parent who cannot be pleased. For some parents, no good behavior is ever good enough. No matter what the child does, there is no way that he or she can ever succeed in the parent's eyes. John Maxwell shares a touching illustration about this in his book *Be a People Person*. In the story, a mother was concerned about her son and went to see a counselor. Her husband had died, and she had hoped that her oldest son would assume the family business when he came of age. However, he refused to accept the responsibility and instead chose to enter a different field.

The mother was hoping that the counselor could convince her son to change his mind. So, the doctor agreed to see him. When he began to probe into the reason why the son didn't want to follow in his father's footsteps, the young man said:

> I would have loved to take over the family business, but you don't understand the relationship I had with my father. He was a driven man who came up the hard way. His objective was to

teach me self-reliance, but he made a drastic mistake. He tried to teach me that principle in a negative way. He thought the best way to teach me self-reliance was to never encourage or praise me. He wanted me to be tough and independent. Every day we played catch in the yard. The object was for me to catch the ball ten straight times. I would catch that ball eight or nine times, but always on that tenth throw he would do everything possible to make me miss it. He would throw it on the ground or over my head but always so I had no chance of catching it.

After saying this, the young man stopped and looked at the counselor. "He never let me catch the tenth ball," he said. "I guess that's why I have to get away from his business; I want to catch that tenth ball!"[87]

Solomon wrote, "When I was my father's son, tender and the only one in the sight of my mother, he also taught me, and said to me: 'Let your heart retain my words'" (Proverbs 4:3-4). Be wise and tenderhearted toward your kids. Teach them in a way that builds their confidence, and they will retain your instruction. Let your kid catch the tenth ball!

Celebrate with Your Kids

Patrick Peyton is believed to have been the first to coin the phrase, "The family that *prays* together stays together."[88] While that is all well and good, the original slogan from a 1954 article in *Parents*

---

[87] John C. Maxwell, *Be a People Person: Effective Leadership Through Effective Relationships* (Colorado Springs, CO: Cook, 2013).
[88] "Patrick Peyton," Wikipedia.org. http://en.wikipedia.org/wiki/Patrick_Peyton

magazine is also quite true: "The family that *plays* together stays together."[89] Christian families should have fun together.

Solomon sums it up this way: "A merry heart does good, like medicine, but a broken spirit dries the bones" (Proverbs 17:22). In other words, joy is good for us—it is like medicine for curing our ills. Contemporary research backs up this claim from the Bible. "I believe that if people can get more laughter in their lives, they are a lot better off," says psychologist Steve Wilson. "They might be healthier too."

While researchers do not know if it is the actual act of laughing that makes us feel better, the evidence shows that we undergo a physiological change when we laugh. Laughter stretches muscles in our faces and bodies, elevates our pulse and blood pressure, and sends more oxygen into our tissues. There is even evidence that it offers some of the same advantages as a physical workout.[90]

My (Steve) kids are my best friends, and we love to hang out. We love to spend time just doing life with one another. We don't just watch religious movies and go to prayer meetings—we laugh a lot and just have fun. We enjoy going on vacation together. I would like my kids even if they were not my kids!

Wise parents recognize the importance of having fun together as a family. They know when to kick back and celebrate with their children. They don't just *pray* together but also *play* together.

---

[89] Linda Brendle, "The Family that _____ Together, Stays Together?" Red Letter Christians, July 29, 2012. http://www.redletterchristians.org/the-family-that-stays-together/

[90] R. Morgan Griffin, "Give Your Body a Boost—with Laugher," WebMD, April 10, 2008. http://www.webmd.com/balance/features/give-your-body-boost-with-laughter

Gradually Let Go of the Leash

The apostle Paul said, "When I was a child, I spoke as a child, I understood as a child, I thought as a child; but when I became a man, I put away childish things" (1 Corinthians 13:11). The ultimate goal of all parenting is to gradually train children so they can function as independent adults. It is about slowly letting go of the leash so they can learn to do more and more on their own.

At first we do everything for our children, because they are simply not able to function on their own. However, as they grow, it is important for us to step back and let them assume more responsibility so that one day they will be able to do everything by themselves. We have to turn them loose and see what they can do. Who knows, they might amaze us! Too many parents today underestimate the abilities of their children.

Back in high school, a friend and I (Josh) used to like to ski in fresh powder, so we planned our skiing trips around storms. We always tried to be on the slopes just after a big snowstorm. Sometimes we didn't get the timing quite right. One time, we got stuck in a terrible snowstorm. The snow was falling heavy, and we could hardly see the road.

I pulled over and called my dad. "What should I do?" I asked. "Should we stop and get a hotel for the night? Should we push on? We might be stuck up here for days. I don't know . . . it looks pretty bad."

I will never forget my dad's response: "I have no idea, son."

"What's that again?" I asked.

"I have no idea," he said. "I am not up there. You are. You are looking at the storm. Make the best decision you can. Be safe!" Click.

I officially felt pushed out of the nest.

As I now think about this story from the viewpoint of a parent, I am certain that my dad was more worried than he let on. However, he wisely knew that it was time for me to make my own decision. If I was old enough to make the trip, I was old enough to decide what to do when the storm came.

Wise parents follow a simple rule: *Never do for your children what your children can do for themselves.* They also follow a corollary to this rule: *Never make a decision for your children that they can make for themselves.* In the end, parenting is not about you. It is about your children. So give your children some room to make their own decisions—and learn from the consequences.

Get Wise!

In his book *Glimpses of Heaven,* author John Ortberg writes about how many of us are "helicopter parents." We like to swoop into our kids' lives and rescue them from anyone who would dare mistreat them or disappoint them. We want them only to experience sunny skies and unobstructed success. He writes:

> One Halloween a mom came to our door to trick or treat. Why didn't she send her kid? Well, the weather's a little bad, she said; she was driving so he didn't have to walk in the mist. But why not send him to the door? Well, he had fallen asleep in the car, she said, so she didn't want him to have to wake up. I felt like saying, "Why don't you eat all his candy and get his stom-

achache for him too—then he can be completely protected!"[91]

Wise parents recognize the difficulties of parenting but don't allow that knowledge to paralyze them. They discipline their kids when necessary, but they do so in a way that teaches them about life and builds their self-esteem. They understand their children, reach out to them, and celebrate life with them. They also let their kids go when the time is right and allow them to make their own decisions.

Don't be foolish when it comes to your children. Train up your kids in the way they should go—in the way the Bible instructs—so they will not depart from it. You will be thankful when the time comes for them to leave the nest.

---

[91] John Ortberg, *Glimpses of Heaven: Surprising Stories of Hope and Encouragement* (Eugene, OR: Harvest House, 2013).

Wise Up About Health

God did a new thing in my (Steve's) life a few years ago in the area of fitness. As I mentioned in chapter 6, I was more than 100 pounds overweight. I had diabetes, high blood pressure, and high cholesterol. I was killing myself with food.

I played football all through high school and college. When I graduated from college, I made a bad decision. I was so tired of the constant workouts that I decided to never exercise again. Sadly, I kept this commitment for many years. Paul says, "For he who sows to his flesh will of the flesh reap corruption" (Galatians 6:8). I sowed, and I reaped. Ultimately, I weighed in at 340 pounds.

Fortunately, God got a hold of me and helped me to wise up about my health. He convicted me that my body was a temple of the Holy Spirit (see 1 Corinthians 6:19) and I was trashing it. I listened to his voice, lost 100 pounds, and eliminated the three diseases from which I was suffering. Praise God, who can change lives![92]

God did a work in Josh's life as well. He had lived most of his life 50 pounds overweight, but God brought influences into his life, including meeting Steve Reynolds, that changed his mindset. Today, he is 50 pounds lighter and has never felt better. He believes

---

[92] For more on my story, see Steve Reynolds, *Bod 4 God: The Four Keys to Weight Loss* (Ventura, CA: Regal, 2010).

in the motto: "No cheesecake tastes as good as fit feels."[93] Josh and I changed, and you can change as well.

Some people ask me if God cares about fitness. It is true that he doesn't care about it as much as our souls. Spiritual training is more important than our physical training. Reading the Word is more important than running. Praying is more important than working out. In 1 Timothy 4:8, Paul writes, "Physical training is of some value, but godliness has value for all things, holding promise for both the present life and the life to come" (NIV). However, fitness *is* still important to God.

In Luke, we read that Jesus not only grew spiritually but also "in wisdom and stature, and in favor with God and men" (2:52, NIV). He grew physically, spiritually, socially, and relationally. He grew in a balanced way. In 3 John 1:2, the disciple John writes, "Dear friend, I pray that you may enjoy good health and that all may go well with you." He was clearly not talking about spiritual health, because in the next line he says, "even as your soul is getting along well" (NIV).

Most churches tend to concern themselves exclusively with spiritual health. As a result, we have a generation of Christians who think godliness has to do with how often they read their Bibles and nothing to do with how often they run. Yet the Bible is clear that God is for physical fitness as well as spiritual fitness. So, if you want to be wise and be like Jesus, grow mentally, spiritually, socially, relationally, *and* physically.

---

[93] For more on Josh's story, see Josh Hunt, *Break a Habit, Make a Habit* (CreateSpace, 2013).

Forget the Past

In Isaiah 43:18, God says, "Do not remember the former things, nor consider the things of old." Your past does not have to be your future, and your present does not have to be your future. So forget the things of the past and move on.

The message of the Bible is that change is possible through the power of the gospel and the transforming work of the Holy Spirit. The past does not have to represent the future. Paul said, "Therefore, if anyone is in Christ, he is a new creation; old things have passed away; behold, all things have become new" (2 Corinthians 5:17). As Max Lucado states, a new creation is "new eyes so we can see by faith. A new mind so we can have the mind of Christ. New strength so we won't grow tired. A new vision so we won't lose heart. A new voice for praise and new hands for service. And most of all, a new heart. A heart that has been cleansed by Christ."[94]

We find this theme throughout the Bible. In Isaiah 43:19, God said, "Behold, I will do a new thing, now it shall spring forth; shall you not know it? I will even make a road in the wilderness and rivers in the desert." Peter stated that God has "caused us to be born again to a living hope" (1 Peter 1:3, NCV). Paul wrote, "Forgetting what is behind and straining toward what is ahead, I press on toward the goal to win the prize for which God has called me heavenward" (Philippians 3:13-14).

Moses is a great example in the Bible of a man who was physically healthy. In Deuteronomy 34:7 we read, "Moses was one hundred and twenty years old when he died. His eyes were not dim nor his natural vigor diminished." Moses not only lived long, but he also

---

[94] Max Lucado, *Everyday Blessings: Inspirational Thoughts from the Published Works of Max Lucado.* (Nashville, TN: Thomas Nelson, Inc., 2004).

lived well. His eyes were not dim nor his vigor diminished. He was strong to the very end of his life.

I (Steve) want to have a long and healthy life. I want to be around for my wife, my children, my grandchildren, and my great grandchildren. I want to be a part of the growing number of Americans who are living to age 100 and beyond.[95] When someone dies, you often hear people say, "It was just their time," but I am not sure this is always true. I think God may have had more in store for that person, but his or her life was cut short because of poor lifestyle choices. There is some mystery here, but it appears that in the sovereignty of God, He extends the lives of those who take better care of themselves.

You can lead a long and healthy life, but you have to forget the past so you can focus on the future. Remember that God says, "I know the plans I have for you . . . plans to prosper you and not to harm you, plans to give you hope and a future" (Jeremiah 29:11). God has plans for your future. So don't get mired down in thoughts that you can never change or that it is too late for you. Press on toward the prize and the life that God has in store for you—and never give up.

Surrender Your Body to God

Once we have let go of the past, we can begin to focus on making changes for the future. The first step in this process is surrendering our bodies to God. Jesus said in Matthew 16:24-25, "If anyone desires to come after Me, let him deny himself, and take up his

---

[95] Studies indicate that the centenarian population in the United States has grown 65.8 percent during the past three decades. See Emily Brandon, "What People Who Live to 100 Have in Common," US News, January 7, 2013. http://money.us-news.com/money/retirement/articles/2013/01/07/what-people-who-live-to-100-have-in-common

cross, and follow Me. For whoever desires to save his life will lose it, but whoever loses his life for My sake will find it." We gain life by surrendering it to God.

In his letter to the Philippians, Paul writes about those who "are the enemies of the cross of Christ: whose end is destruction, whose god is their belly, and whose glory is in their shame—who set their mind on earthly things" (3:18-19). These words were written about me (Steve) and for me. I was an idolater. My god was my belly, and no one was going to tell me what to eat or not eat.

I had to learn that in order to be an obedient follower of Jesus, I needed to deny myself, take up my cross, and follow Christ. I had to go from having a bod for Steve to having a bod for God. Up to that point I had been eating for my own gratification, not for God's glory. It was all about what I wanted to eat and what I wanted to do. I wanted to overeat, and I didn't want to exercise.

God brought me to the realization that I needed to submit to Him and embrace the fact that He should be "magnified in my body" (Philippians 1:20b). Paul's words in 1 Corinthians 10:31 came alive for me: "Therefore, whether you eat or drink, or whatever you do, do all to the glory of God." I needed to start eating and drinking to the glory of God. I needed to admit that I had a spoon problem, and that eating that huge bowl of ice cream before bed every night was not glorifying to God. I needed to admit that I had a fork problem, and that I liked having lots of food on that fork.

In Proverbs 23:20, we read, "Do not join those who drink too much wine or gorge themselves on meat" (NIV). All too often we focus on the "drink too much wine" part and not on the "gorge" part. However, it is clear that surrendering our bodies to God includes surrendering our fork and our spoon. It means treating our bodies like the temple of the Holy Spirit and taking care of our health.

In my case, I didn't have a problem with drugs or alcohol. I didn't have a problem with cigarettes. I was not sexually immoral. But I was sinful just the same because I had a problem with overeating. It was really that simple. So, for you, the question is equally simple: Are you willing to fully surrender your body to God?

Stop Making Excuses

The next step in being wise about our health is to stop making excuses that keep us from realizing our potential. Excuses are as old as the Garden of Eden. After God confronted Adam about his sin, he protested that his sin wasn't really his fault. "Then the man said, 'The woman whom You gave to be with me, she gave me of the tree, and I ate" (Genesis 3:12). Today, the three most common excuses I hear about not getting healthy relate to what I call the three *T*s: time, tired, and taste.

Many people claim they do not have the *time* to eat healthy and exercise. The truth is that if we don't make time for healthy living today, we will have to make time for illness tomorrow. It takes a lot of time to go to doctors and pick up prescriptions so we can sit in our chair and eat ice cream. We are all busy, and yet we all make time for what is important to us. So, if we truly have a conviction that we need to honor God with our bodies, we will find the time.

Another complaint I hear is that people are too *tired* to be healthy. Well, it's true that when we start exercising, we are going to be tired. However, what happens is that as we keep on exercising, we find that we have more energy and feel less tired. I don't much like the routine of exercise, but I do like the results!

Of course, people also complain that they don't like the *taste* of healthy food. "I just don't like vegetables," they say, "and ice cream tastes so good!" I say, "Who cares?" Too much ice cream will kill you. We never read in someone's obituary that obesity was the cause of death—it is always heart disease, stroke, diabetes, cancers—but it's the truth. "John Smith: died of eating too much ice cream." On the other hand, vegetables will cure you. A diet rich in vegetables can actually *reduce* the risk of heart disease, protect against certain types of cancer, and lower blood pressure.[96]

I (Steve) have to admit that I am still tempted to make up excuses. Jesus said, "The spirit indeed is willing, but the flesh is weak" (Matthew 26:41b), and that is certainly my problem. I believe the right things, but it is hard for me to always behave rightly. Cartoonists Don Wilder and Bill Rechin said, "Excuses are the nails used to build a house of failure." Benjamin Franklin put it even more succinctly: "He that is good for making excuses is seldom good for anything else."

We overcome excuses when we shift our mindset and begin to visualize the benefits of leading a healthy lifestyle. When our "why" becomes strong enough, we will find the "how." We will begin to glorify God in our bodies and get the most out of them. In so doing, we will find that we feel better, have more energy, and can do more—for ourselves, our families, and for God. Our minds will work better, because our brains work best in active bodies. Ultimately,

---

[96] "Why Is It Important to Eat Vegetables?" USDA, ChooseMyPlate.gov. http://www.choosemyplate.gov/food-groups/vegetables-why.html

being healthy will make us feel, in the words of author Franklin P. Adams, "that now is the best time of the year."

However, before we can realize all these benefits, we have to wise up and stop making excuses for why we can't get in shape. We have to start making changes.

Start Making Small Changes

Once we have surrendered our bodies to God and gotten rid of the excuses, we are ready to make some small sustainable steps toward change. Note that this doesn't require an extreme makeover—as Zechariah 4:10 says, we should not despise "the day of small things." In my life, I starting making these simple changes that ultimately left me 100 pounds lighter:

- Instead of eating a bagel, I ate a protein health bar
- Instead of eating ice cream, I ate nonfat yogurt
- Instead of drinking diet sodas, I drank water during the day
- Instead of eating a hamburger with fries, I ate a grilled chicken salad with a small amount of low-fat dressing
- Instead of using mayonnaise on sandwiches, I used mustard
- Instead of eating fried chips and dip, I ate baked chips and salsa
- Instead of eating lots of beef, I ate lots of lean chicken and some fish
- Instead of eating white bread, I ate whole-grain bread
- Instead of eating fried foods, I ate baked foods

- Instead of using vegetable oil, I used olive oil
- Instead of using high-fat creamer, I used fat-free creamer

I didn't get unhealthy in a day. It took years for me to get from the place I had been when I graduated from college—being able to lift lots of weight and nearly dunk a basketball—to being overweight. Likewise, I didn't get fit in a day. I took on healthy habits one by one and one day at a time, and gradually I got more and more fit. I learned that my stomach was the size of my fist, so I didn't need to eat meals that were the size of my head.

When the Israelites were preparing to make a change and move from the wilderness into the Promised Land, Moses said to them, "The Lord your God is bringing you into a good land . . . a land of wheat and barley, of vines and fig trees and pomegranates, a land of olive oil and honey; a land in which you will eat bread without scarcity, in which you will lack nothing" (Deuteronomy 8:7-9). God had blessed humans with around 10,000 taste buds, and He wanted His people to enjoy good food.

The same is true for us today. However, notice that I said *good food.* Much of what passes for food today in the typical American's diet is nothing short of poison. In my life, I had to acknowledge that fast food was killing me. No longer would I drive through the drive thru—I would now drive past.

Once I made this shift in my thinking and started to see the pounds drop off, I became motivated to keep going. You will find the same to be true. It is motivating to be able to picture yourself 40 pounds thinner. It is motivating when people comment on how good you look. It is motivating when you can start wearing smaller clothes.

Yet it all takes time, and you need to recognize that is okay. You have to be in it for the long haul and not be satisfied with a fad diet that you can't sustain. You want to make gradual changes, ramp up the exercise, and find a healthy lifestyle that you can consistently sustain.

Find a Diet You Can Sustain

I have found that the solution to losing weight does not come from a pill, a powder, or a potion. It comes from eating more foods from the fresh-food section and less from the junk-food section. It comes from consuming more apples and less apple pie, more oranges and less orange soda, and more bran flakes and less frosted flakes.

The litmus test of any diet is whether you can sustain it the rest of your life. I (Josh) found diets to be very confusing. One would say to start my day with bacon and eggs, and the next day with Cheerios and skim milk. I was not alone in my confusion. Most Americans find it easier to do their taxes than figure out what a healthy diet should look like. However, as I studied these diets more carefully, I discovered something that nearly all of them have in common: they all recommend minimizing bad carbs. These are high glycemic carbs that quickly turn to sugar.

Armed with this knowledge, I found a plan that I believe I can sustain the rest of my life. I call it the "colorful diet," and it allows me to eat as much as I want, avoid counting calories, and never go hungry. Notice I said I can eat as *much* as I want, but not *anything* I want. In particular, I avoid five white (or nearly white) poisons: (1) sugar, (2) wheat, (3) potatoes, (4) white rice, and (5) corn. I eat as many fresh fruits and vegetables as I want, and as much as I want of anything else. This is a diet I can sustain.

138

Exercise More and Get Moving

In Genesis 2:15, God put Adam in the Garden and told him to tend and keep it, not sit and look at it. Sitting is the new smoking. We spend more time sitting than we do sleeping. Our bodies were not made for this—we were made to move. So get up every hour and walk 500 steps. Stretch. Lift something. Run in place. Move.

Again, the path to success will be through baby steps. Take the stairs. Park in the farthest parking space from your office or the store. Take a quick walk around the block before you head into the house. Do something to get your blood pumping, your muscles working, and your feet moving.

Isaiah writes, "Those who wait on the LORD shall renew their strength; they shall mount up with wings like eagles, they shall run and not be weary, they shall walk and not faint" (40:31). There is a God in heaven who can renew your strength. He can help you run and not be weary. He can help you walk and not faint. The secret is to "wait on the Lord," which is another way of saying to depend on God.

If you want to run, and you want to walk, and you want to get moving to improve your health, know that there is a God in heaven who is eager to support you. Rely on Him and He "shall supply all your need according to His riches in glory by Christ Jesus" (Philippians 4:19).

Get Wise!

According to the Centers for Disease Control and Prevention, 69 percent of adults in America are overweight. Thirty-five percent of those adults are also obese.[97] That represents a huge percentage of our population—and a huge percentage of our health care costs. Much of this is due to people eating too much and moving too little.

This doesn't have to be true of you. You can be a part of the 31 percent of people who are leading healthy lifestyles. You can wise up about your health and fitness. You can decide to move past your previous mistakes, go forward, and surrender your body to God. You can choose to stop making excuses and start making small changes. You can find a diet that you can sustain and make a commitment to exercise more.

Be wise when it comes to your health, and remember that the past does not equal the future.

[97] "Obesity and Overweight," Centers for Disease Control, 2011–2012 data. http://www.cdc.gov/nchs/fastats/obesity-overweight.htm

Wise Up About Godliness

Solomon saved the best for last. In the final chapter in the book of Proverbs, he includes sayings about the qualities of "the virtuous wife." Although the message is targeted toward women, it also applies to men who want to be godly, men looking for a godly wife, and husbands who want to know how to support their wives. In other words, it is a message for any person who wants to wise up about godliness.

In Proverbs 31:10, we read, "Who can find a virtuous wife? For her worth is far above rubies." We learn two things from this verse: (1) a godly woman is valuable, and (2) she is hard to find. Fortunately, I (Steve) have had three godly women who have helped to shape my life. In Proverbs 31:28, we read that we are to rise up and call such women blessed, so I would like to do that in this chapter.

The first woman was my grandmother, Emma Reynolds. During my early years our family went to her house every Sunday afternoon after church, and we spent the day together. It was a great time of food, family, and fellowship. During the summers, I spent about a month with Grandma Emma. She taught me to fish, and her sons taught me to hunt. She was sweet, and she was also godly. Every night before we went to bed, she would pull out her well worn King James Bible and read to me. Every night, she would pour the Word of God into my life. I would not be the man I am today if it were not for the influence of Emma Reynolds. She was a Proverbs 31 woman, and I call her blessed.

The second woman was my mom, Elizabeth Reynolds. She has given her life to her family. I know there will be a small crowd at her funeral because she was not a public figure, but she deeply loves her family and is deeply loved by her family. She is a shining example of what it means to be a Proverbs 31 woman. She is a hard worker who prioritizes her family. So much of who I am today comes from my mom.

My mom is a simple woman. Her mom died when she was young, so she had to cook for her family and take on the role of being the woman of the house. She is not well educated, but she has made a difference through her life and her prayers. It is because of her influence that she has two sons and two grandsons today who are preaching the gospel. Every morning she gets up early and prays for each of us. I rise up and call her blessed.

The third woman who has shaped my life is my wife, Debbie. Only heaven will reveal the sacrifices that she has made for the Kingdom. A woman's greatest need is security, yet when I felt called to move to northern Virginia to start a new church, she gladly supported this decision. The vast majority of church plants fail, yet she willingly followed. She has supported me in every way possible.

I was a lousy husband for many years. (I am still not that good!) For many years I was an extreme workaholic. I worked six and a half days each week and patted myself on the back for having one family night off a week. That is a sin. God commands us to "remember the Sabbath day, to keep it holy" (Exodus 20:8), and take a day off every week. I didn't, and Debbie put up with it. Debbie is the heart of our family. She is the reason why we have wonderful, godly children. I call her blessed.

So, what does it take to be a godly person? What does it take to be wise in this area? The final chapter in Proverbs provides us with some clues.

Be Diligent

"She seeks wool and flax, and willingly works with her hands. She is like the merchant ships, she brings her food from afar. She also rises while it is yet night, and provides food for her household, and a portion for her maidservants. She considers a field and buys it; from her profits she plants a vineyard. She girds herself with strength, and strengthens her arms" (Proverbs 31:13-17).

There are a couple of items to notice in this list. First, in verse 13, we read that she works "willingly." The Hebrew word for this term appears 38 times in the Old Testament and is translated 21 different ways in the *New King James Version*. According to one commentary, it means "delight, pleasure, or desire."[98] The *New American Standard Bible* conveys this idea: "Works with her hands in delight." She doesn't just work willingly but joyfully and eagerly. She also "rises while it is yet night" (verse 15). She is fired up to go to work and rises early to start her day.

As previously discussed, we live in a thank-God-it's-Friday type world. Most of us can't wait for the weekend so we don't have to work. We don't like to rise in the light of the morning, much less while it is still night. However, the godly person works diligently and cheerfully. They thank God it's Monday so they can go to work and provide for their families.

---

[98] Warren Baker and Eugene E. Carpenter, *The Complete Word Study Dictionary: Old Testament* (Chattanooga, TN: AMG Publishers, 2003), p. 365.

In Ecclesiastes 9:10, Solomon states, "Whatever your hand finds to do, do it with your might." That is what godly people do. They work hard, work joyfully, and work diligently. They are wise and follow Paul's instructions in Colossians 3:23: "Whatever you do, do it heartily, as to the Lord and not to men."

Be Trustworthy

"The heart of her husband safely trusts her; so he will have no lack of gain" (Proverbs 31:11). Author and pastor Paul Tripp defines trust as being so convinced that you can rely on the integrity, strength, character, and faithfulness of another person that you are willing to place yourself in his or her care.[99] That is what Lemuel, the author of Proverbs 31, is referring to here.

Trust is one of the essential foundation stones of marriage. If there is no trust, there is no marriage—at least, not the kind of marriage that God designed when he created the institution. Two people can live together and have relational détente without trust. However, without it they cannot have the intimate, vulnerable, mutually cooperative, one-flesh union that marriage is intended to be.

We have to be able to take our spouses at face value. We have to be comfortable when the other person is not in our eyesight. We can't be worrying about whether they are being honest or if they will be faithful to their promises. We can't live with the fear that they care more for themselves than they care for us or wonder if someone else has captured their affections. We can't exist in a relationship where we fear for our safety, or cannot be vulnerable, or have

---

[99] Paul David Tripp, *What Did You Expect? Redeeming the Realities of Marriage* (Wheaton, IL: Crossway, 2010).

concerns the person will take advantage of us. We cannot be in such a situation where godliness is not present.

Trust is about rest, peace, security, and hope. It allows us to face the worst in our relationships and hope for the best. It enables us to take risks and makes it safe for us to share our feelings. It allows us to speak honestly and listen honestly. It lets us know that we are cared for and that we are safe to voice our concerns. It prompts us to look out for our spouses' interests and rest in the knowledge that they will look out for us.

Godly people are trustworthy people. They are true to their word and committed to doing only what is good. They do everything they can to let their spouses (and others) know that they can entrust themselves to their care.

Be Shrewd

"She considers a field and buys it; from her profits she plants a vineyard. . . . She perceives that her merchandise is good, and her lamp does not go out by night" (Proverbs 31:16,18). As we discussed in chapter 8, godly people not only work hard but also work smart. They consider—which has the sense of devise, plot, think about, or give careful attention to—a plan before they jump into it. They don't just decide to buy something major on a whim. They do their homework first.

In Matthew 25:14-30, Jesus told the parable of a man who went away on a journey and entrusted three of his servants with some money to invest. The first and second servants were wise and doubled their master's investment. The third was foolish and did nothing with it. When the master returned, he praised his first two servants and made them rulers over many things. But to his third servant he said:

> You wicked and lazy servant, you knew that I reap where I have not sown, and gather where I have not scattered seed. So you ought to have deposited my money with the bankers, and at my coming I would have received back my own with interest. Therefore take the talent from him, and give it to him who has ten talents (verses 27-28).

Godly people are wise with the gifts they have been given. They don't squander their resources or hide them in the ground. They are "shrewd as snakes and as innocent as doves" (Matthew 10:16, NIV).

Be Generous

"She extends her hand to the poor, yes, she reaches out her hands to the needy" (Proverbs 31:20). If we want to be wise, we must not only be shrewd with our investments but also generous with our giving. In the Old Testament, God told the people, "If there is among you a poor man of your brethren, within any of the gates in your land which the LORD your God is giving you, you shall not harden your heart nor shut your hand from your poor brother" (Deuteronomy 15:7). God commanded His people to be generous with what He had given to them.

The great thing about generosity is that it is not only good for the recipient but also good for the giver. Generosity benefits everyone. In fact, research shows that it reduces stress, makes us happier, makes us more successful, improves our relationships, and may even increase our lifespan.[100] Solomon captures idea this when he

---

[100] Lisa Firestone, "The Benefits of Generosity," Huffington Post, June 13, 2014. http://www.huffingtonpost.com/2013/12/01/generosity-health_n_4323727.html

writes, "There is one who scatters, yet increases more; and there is one who withholds more than is right, but it leads to poverty. The generous soul will be made rich, and he who waters will also be watered himself" (Proverbs 11:24-25).

Godly people are generous people. They recognize that everything they have been given in this life comes from God. They are wise to share their resources with others as God has commanded them to do.

Be Forward Thinking

"She is not afraid of snow for her household, for all her household is clothed with scarlet" (Proverbs 31:21). Wise people prepare for what they *know* is coming in the future. They are not taken unaware when the snow falls and the weather turns cold. They don't have to worry about how their little ones will stay warm, because they have planned ahead for their families' needs. They clothe their household with "scarlet," which suggests high-quality clothing that will protect from the winter frost.

Wise people also make plans for what they *don't know* is ahead. There is always some form of "winter" in our lives. Cars break down. Heaters need repair. Refrigerators have to be replaced. Wise people set some money aside for these emergencies. They are ready for anything. As the saying goes, "It wasn't raining when Noah built the ark."

In Matthew 7:24-28, Jesus told another parable that captures this idea. There were two men who were building their houses. The first man, who was wise, built his house on a rock. The second man, who was foolish, built his house on the sand. When the rains of winter came and the floods rose, the house founded on the rock did not fall. But the house founded on the sand was washed away.

Godly people are forward thinking when it comes to thinking about the needs of those who depend upon them. They plan ahead and build on the rock. They have a long-time perspective.

Be Confident

"Strength and honor are her clothing; she shall rejoice in time to come" (Proverbs 31:25). The *New International Version* reads, "she can laugh at days to come." The *Contemporary English Version* reads, "she is cheerful about the future." Godly people are confident because they know they are walking on the right path, have integrity, and are prepared for the future. They don't get their feathers ruffled easily.

James Dobson once conducted a survey about the major causes of depression in women and found that low self-esteem was at the top of the list. He noted, "The 'disease' of inferiority has reached epidemic proportions among females, particularly at this time in our history."[101] Other studies show that "over time, low self-esteem is a risk factor for depression, regardless of who is tested and how. . . . Low self-esteem causes depression but not vice versa. Therefore, if a person has low self-esteem, there's an increased risk of developing depression."[102]

---

[101] James C. Dobson, *What Wives Wish Their Husbands Knew About Women* (Carol Stream, IL: Tyndale, 2010).
[102] Elizabeth Venzin, "Is Low Self-Esteem Making You Vulnerable to Depression?" Psych Central, March 29, 2014. http://psychcentral.com/blog/archives/2014/03/29/is-low-self-esteem-making-you-vulnerable-to-depression/

Not so the woman in Proverbs 31. She holds her chin high in confidence. Godly people carry the same confidence with them through life.

Appreciate Beauty

"She makes tapestry for herself; her clothing is fine linen and purple" (Proverbs 31:22). Visit the home of the average bachelor and you will find what looks like a warehouse—stark, undecorated, and plain surroundings. Men, by nature, require three pair of shoes: one for running, one that is black, and one that is brown. Women, by nature, require . . . well, who knows how many shoes women require.

The reason has to do with a woman's sense of style. The Proverbs 31 woman is no exception. She makes a tapestry for herself. Why? Because it is pretty. Nor is her inner beauty and outer beauty mutually exclusive. Just because she is godly doesn't mean she has to dress like a frump. She could perhaps relate to Maria from *West Side Story* who sang, "I feel pretty!"

Why does she clothe herself in purple? Author Elizabeth George provides several possible reasons:

- For warmth: Red or scarlet clothing (meaning "to shine") indicates that it retained heat. Note that wool had to be dyed the color scarlet, and to become truly scarlet, wool had to be dipped in the dye more than once.
- For stately appearance: Because of the dye and the added labor and time, scarlet robes were luxurious and costly. Scarlet was the color of kings' clothing and signified dignity, luxury, and magnificence.

- For quality: Only the best will do for this beautiful woman's family. The fact that they are clothed with wool—and with scarlet wool at that—speaks of the quality clothing she provides. Then, as now, few people owned more than one woolen overcoat.

- For durability: You've certainly felt the difference between cheap, thin wool and wool that is rich and heavy. One meaning of the Hebrew word for scarlet is "double." This woman would only make quality, double thick clothing, extending a double blessing to her brood.[103]

There is an even greater lesson here: godly people appreciate the beautiful things that God has placed in their lives. They give thanks to God for His blessings and don't take people or things for granted. Like David, they recognize that "the heavens declare the glory of God, and the firmament shows His handiwork" (Psalm 19:1).

Give Compliments

"Her children arise and call her blessed; her husband also, and he praises her" (Proverbs 31:28, NIV). Mark Twain once said, "I can live for two months on a good compliment." I think most of us are that way. We all need a good compliment from time to time. Yet often we are too slow to give a sincere compliment to another person.

Godly people don't hesitate when it comes to praising another person for something he or she has done well. They focus more on others than on themselves. They take Jesus' words in John 13:34

---

[103] Elizabeth George, *Beautiful in God's Eyes: The Treasures of the Proverbs 31* Woman (Eugene, OR: Harvest House, 2005).

to heart: "A new commandment I give to you, that you love one another; as I have loved you, that you also love one another." They catch their spouses and their children doing something right and praise them for it.

At the beginning of this chapter, I told you of three women in my life whom I call blessed: my grandmother, Emma Reynolds; my mom, Elizabeth Reynolds; and my wife, Debbie Reynolds. These were godly women who encouraged me, prayed for me, and stood by me. My life would not have been the same without their influence.

What godly women in your life do you wish to rise up and declare blessed? What would a sincere compliment from you mean to them? Make an effort to tell them. Call your mother and tell her how much you appreciate her. Write a card to your spouse and say how much you appreciate him or her. Send an email to a friend to thank him or her for just being a part of your life. Don't wait for a special day to arrive.

Get Wise!

"She opens her mouth with wisdom, and on her tongue is the law of kindness" (Proverbs 31:26). One commentator said these words suggest the Proverbs 31 woman understands that her mouth does not have to be constantly open. She can be quiet when she has nothing to say. However, when she speaks, people listen to her because she is a woman of wise words.

Can people say the same of you? Do they see you as a wise person or as somewhat foolish? Can you honestly say that you value godly wisdom above all other things in life? How are you turning to God and relying on His wisdom in your decision making, your communication, your friendships, and your conflicts, your intimate relations with your spouse, your struggles, your finances, your work, your parenting, and your health? As you go through your day, are you continually asking yourself the best question ever: "Is it wise?"

It is our hope that you will pursue wisdom all your days so that "it may go well with you" (Ephesians 6:3). Always remember that if you find you lack wisdom, you can "ask of God, who gives to all liberally and without reproach" (James 1:5). You can call to the God of the universe and He "will answer you, and will tell you great and hidden things that you have not known" (Jeremiah 33:3, ESV). Allow His wisdom to fill you and guide you so that you can say with the psalmist, "Your word is a lamp to my feet and a light to my path" (Psalm 119:105).

Continue to get wisdom. Desire it. Prize it. Work for it. Look for it in others. Thank God for it, and give Him the glory when He shows you how to use it.

How to Become a Christian

You're not here by accident. God loves you. He wants you to have a personal relationship with Him through Jesus, His Son. There is just one thing that separates you from God. That one thing is sin.

The Bible describes sin in many ways. Most simply, sin is our failure to measure up to God's holiness and His righteous standards. We sin by things we do, choices we make, attitudes we show, and thoughts we entertain. We also sin when we fail to do right things. The Bible affirms our own experience – "there is none righteous, not even one." No matter how good we try to be, none of us does right things all the time.

People tend to divide themselves into groups - good people and bad people. But God says that every person who has ever lived is a sinner, and that any sin separates us from God. No matter how we might classify ourselves, this includes you and me. We are all sinners.

> "For all have sinned and come short of the glory of God."
> Romans 3:23

Many people are confused about the way to God. Some think they will be punished or rewarded according to how good they are. Some think they should make things right in their lives before they try to come to God. Others find it hard to understand how Jesus could love them when other people don't seem to. But I have great news for you! God DOES love you! More than you can ever imagine! And there's nothing you can do to make Him stop! Yes, our sins demand punishment - the punishment of death and separation from God. But, because of His great love, God sent His only Son Jesus to die for our sins.

"God demonstrates His own love for us in this: While we were still sinners, Christ died for us." Romans 5:8

For you to come to God you have to get rid of your sin problem. But, in our own strength, not one of us can do this! You can't make yourself right with God by being a better person. Only God can rescue us from our sins. He is willing to do this not because of anything you can offer Him, but JUST BECAUSE HE LOVES YOU!

> "He saved us, not because of righteous things we had done, but because of His mercy." Titus 3:5

It's God's grace that allows you to come to Him - not your efforts to "clean up your life" or work your way to Heaven. You can't earn it. It's a free gift.

> "For it is by grace you have been saved, through faith - and this not from yourselves, it is the gift of God - not by works, so that no one can boast." Ephesians 2:8-9

For you to come to God, the penalty for your sin must be paid. God's gift to you is His son, Jesus, who paid the debt for you when He died on the Cross.

> "For the wages of sin is death, but the gift of God is eternal life in Jesus Christ our Lord." Romans 6:23

Jesus paid the price for your sin and mine by giving His life on a cross at a place called Calvary, just outside of the city walls of

Jerusalem in ancient Israel. God brought Jesus back from the dead. He provided the way for you to have a personal relationship with Him through Jesus. When we realize how deeply our sin grieves the heart of God and how desperately we need a Savior, we are ready to receive God's offer of salvation. To admit we are sinners means turning away from our sin and selfishness and turning to follow Jesus. The Bible word for this is "repentance" - to change our thinking about how grievous sin is, so our thinking is in line with God's.

All that's left for you to do is to accept the gift that Jesus is holding out for you right now.

> "If you confess with your mouth, "Jesus is Lord," and believe in your heart that God raised him from the dead, you will be saved. For it is with your heart that you believe and are justified, and it is with your mouth that you confess and are saved." Romans 10:9-10

God says that if you believe in His son, Jesus, you can live forever with Him in glory.

> "For God so loved the world that He gave his one and only Son, that whoever believes in him shall not perish, but have eternal life." John 3:16

Are you ready to accept the gift of eternal life that Jesus is offering you right now? Let's review what this commitment involves:

> I acknowledge I am a sinner in need of a Savior - this is to repent or turn away from sin

I believe in my heart that God raised Jesus from the dead - this is to trust that Jesus paid the full penalty for my sins

I confess Jesus as my Lord and my God - this is to surrender control of my life to Jesus

I receive Jesus as my Savior forever - this is to accept that God has done for me and in me what He promised

If it is your sincere desire to receive Jesus into your heart as your personal Lord and Savior, then talk to God from your heart:

Here's a Suggested Prayer:

"Lord Jesus, I know that I am a sinner and I do not deserve eternal life. But, I believe You died and rose from the grave to make me a new creation and to prepare me to dwell in your presence forever. Jesus, come into my life, take control of my life, forgive my sins and save me. I am now placing my trust in You alone for my salvation and I accept your free gift of eternal life."

This presentation is courtesy
http://www.sbc.net/knowjesus/theplan.asp

Wise Up With Your Church

Study *Wise Up!* with your whole church! Pulpit Press provides the following resources available to you to build an all-church campaign:

- Steve Reynold's original sermons that were the basis of this book.

- This book.

- *Wise Up! Good Questions Have Groups Talking*, by Josh Hunt . This is a small group leader's guide for your teachers. Available on Amazon.com

For more information, see www.pulpit-press.com

Made in the USA
San Bernardino, CA
17 March 2016